THE OFFICIAL SOVIET
MOSIN-NAGANT
RIFLE
MANUAL

Operating Instructions for the
Model 1891/30 Rifle and Model
1938 and Model 1944 Carbines

Originally Issued by the Ministry of Defense of the U.S.S.R.

With Original Illustrations and Translation by
Maj. James F. Gebhardt, U.S. Army (Retired)

Paladin Press • Boulder, Colorado

Also by James F. Gebhardt

The Official SKS Manual

The Official Soviet AKM Manual

The Official Soviet Army Hand Grenade Manual

The Official Soviet SVD Manual

The Official Soviet 7.62mm Handgun Manual

The Official Soviet Mosin-Nagant Rifle Manual
by James F. Gebhardt

Copyright © 2000 by James F. Gebhardt

ISBN 1-58160-081-X
Printed in the United States of America

Published by Paladin Press, a division of
Paladin Enterprises, Inc., P.O. Box 1307,
Boulder, Colorado 80306, USA.
(303) 443-7250

Direct inquiries and/or orders to the above address.

Originally published in the Soviet Union under the title *Nastavleniye po strelkovomu delu: vin-
tovka obr. 1891/30 g. i karabiny obr. 1938 g. i obr. 1944 g.* under the editorial supervision of
Col. I.K. Vilchinskiy, technical editor R.L. Solomonik, proofreader T.I. Khryastova, by the
Military Press of the Ministry of Defense of the USSR, Moscow, 1961.

Visit our Web site at www.paladin-press.com

Table of Contents

PART TWO

METHODS AND INSTRUCTIONS FOR FIRING THE RIFLE

About this book

After translating Soviet Army manuals for a long list of Russian and Soviet pistols, submachine guns, machine guns, and rifles, I have come back to the most basic of Russian and Soviet small arms—the Mosin-Nagant bolt-action rifle. I was fortunate to obtain from Yuri Evgenov in St. Petersburg, Russia, a like-new copy of the Soviet Army manual for this rifle, published in 1961.

I am departing from my custom in previous manuals of extracting several paragraphs of historical information for translation and presentation in this space. Instead, I refer the reader to a recently published work, *The Mosin-Nagant Rifle*, by Terence W. Lapin (North Cape Publications, 1998). Mr. Lapin has done an excellent job in researching and presenting historical material pertaining to all models of the Mosin-Nagant bolt-action rifle, irrespective of variant, country of origin, or modification. With his discussion of markings Mr. Lapin has also provided an excellent reference work for the Mosin-Nagant rifle and carbine collector.

Enthusiasts of the Mosin-Nagant rifle will also find much of value in this manual. But my greatest hope is that shooters of the Mosin-Nagant rifle will use the information found in these pages to enjoy their Mosin-Nagant rifle or carbine at its best, on the range or in the field. Whether it is in disassembly and assembly, cleaning and lubricating, or firing for zero at the specified zeroing range of 100 meters, this manual describes in intricate detail all the steps, procedures, and criteria that will ensure proper and safe function of the rifle or carbine.

Near the back of the manual are several data tables that describe the ballistic performance of the 148-grain type-1908 projectile and the weight and length of the basic rifle and carbines in various configurations.

For those who have or aspire to the sniper version of this rifle, an appendix is included that describes both the PE and PU scopes, and the procedures and criteria for zeroing the sniper rifle without and with scope.

Finally, I would like to alert the reader to a technical term used in the manuscript that is familiar to everyone but not in the context of this rifle. This term is "*kurok*" in Russian, which I prefer to translate as "hammer" vice the more conventional "cocking piece." The hammer, or "cocking piece" if you prefer, is mounted in the rear portion of the bolt assembly. It has a round knurled knob on the back, with a threaded hole through the center into which the rear end of the firing pin is screwed. The knob is used to cock the hammer or to rotate it to the left to the "safe" position.

In sum, whether you are a collector or shooter of the venerable Mosin-Nagant rifle or a variant thereof, you will find much in this manual that is useful, if not essential to the safe enjoyment of your firearm.

About the translator

James F. Gebhardt is a retired U.S. Army officer who served as an enlisted infantryman, armor officer, and Soviet foreign area officer during a 20-year career. Gebhardt studied the Russian language at the University of Idaho, the University of Washington, Defense Language Institute (Monterey), and the U.S. Army Russian Institute in Garmisch, Germany. He has performed military duty in the Soviet Union, and escorted Soviet scientific, diplomatic, and military personnel on U.S. military installations in the United States.

Mr. Gebhardt is the author or translator of several previous works in the military history field, with a focus on memoirs of Soviet Army and Navy veterans of World War II. His latest published work, *Fighting for the Soviet Motherland: Recollections From the Eastern Front* (Lincoln: University of Nebraska Press), by Dmitriy Loza, was selected by the History Book Club in January 1999. He recently submitted for publication a manuscript that describes the employment of the Bell P-39 Airacobra by the Red Air Force, and is now translating a manuscript that describes the tactical and technical history of the BM-10 and BM-13 Katyusha multiple rocket launcher systems used by the Red Army in World War II.

The Official Soviet Mosin-Nagant Rifle Manual is James Gebhardt's sixth Paladin Press weapons manual.

Introduction

Combat Characteristics and Nomenclature of the Rifle and Carbines

1. The **rifle** (Figure 1) is the basic weapon of the rifleman for destruction of the enemy by fire, bayonet, and butt stroke. It is the most effective means of defeating individual personnel targets (exposed, camouflaged, moving, and fleeting).

Figure 1. General view of the rifle

The best results are obtained with the rifle when fired at ranges up to 400 meters. Concentrated fire of riflemen is used to defeat group targets at ranges up to 1000 meters. Fire at low-flying aircraft and parachutists is conducted at ranges up to 500 meters.

Snipers defeat targets at ranges out to 800 meters.

2. The rifle is simple in construction and handling, durable, and reliable in function. It is always ready for quick action.

3. The combat rate of fire of the rifle is 10 shots per minute.

4. The maximum range of firing from this rifle is 2,000 meters. The maximum range of the type-1908 projectile is 3,000 meters.

5. In addition to the Model 1891/30 rifle, riflemen are armed with the Model 1938 and Model 1944 carbines.

The **Model 1938 carbine** differs in construction from the Model 1891/30 rifle only in that it has a short barrel and less weight (see appendix 2). In addition, the carbine does not have a bayonet.

The **Model 1944 carbine** differs from the Model 1938 carbine only in that it has an attached, folding bayonet. The bayonet has two positions: **combat**–the bayonet is deployed to the forward position and prepared for use in hand-to-hand combat; and **travel**–the bayonet is folded to the rear and its cutting edge lies along the upper right edge of the stock forearm.

The reduced weight and length (and in the Model 1944 carbine also the presence of the folding bayonet) make the carbine, relative to the rifle, more convenient in combat use, particularly during actions in trenches, buildings, wooded areas, and also when overcoming various obstacles and barricades. The maximum firing range of the carbine is 1,000 meters. In all other combat characteristics and nomenclature, the carbines are the same as the Model 1891/30 rifle.

The instructions contained in this manual regarding the construction, handling, maintenance, and preservation of the rifle, and also the methods and instructions for firing from the rifle apply in equal measure to the Model 1938 and Model 1944 carbines. The peculiarities associated with insignificant differences in construction and ballistic data of the carbines are noted in appropriate paragraphs of these instructions.

Part One

CONSTRUCTION, HANDLING, MAINTENANCE, AND PRESERVATION OF THE RIFLE

Chapter I

CONSTRUCTION OF THE RIFLE

Description of the Rifle's Components

Barrel

6. The **barrel** (Figure 2) guides the flight of the bullet. Internally the barrel **bore** has four grooves with a clockwise twist. The **grooves** impart rotational motion to the bullet during flight. The spaces between the grooves are called **lands**. The distance (in diameter) between two opposite lands is the **caliber** of the barrel bore, 7.62 millimeters.

Figure 2. Barrel with receiver

1 - rear sight   2 - front sight

 The rear portion of the bore is smooth; it serves to house the cartridge and is called the **chamber**. The chamber is joined with the rifled portion of the barrel bore by means of the **bullet chamber**.

 Externally, at the muzzle end, the barrel has a front sight base. A **rear-sight base** is affixed to the rear portion of the barrel. Above the chamber are stamped a [serial] number, [ordnance] mark, and the year of production of the rifle.

 The enlarged breach portion of the barrel ends in a threaded **tenon**, by which the barrel is tightly screwed into the **receiver**. On the face of this tenon is a **taper**, along which the extractor claw slides during rotation of the bolt.

 The Model 1944 carbine has a securely attached immovable tube at the muzzle end that serves as a mounting base for the bayonet (see Figure 27). At the front end and on top of this tube is the front sight base. On the right side of the rear end of this tube is a boss with brackets for mounting the bayonet. The brackets have holes for installing a large screw that serves as the trunnion for rotation of the bayonet during its unfolding and folding.

 The brackets have tapered cams on the rear surfaces for securing the folding bayonet in the travel (folded) position. The front surfaces of the brackets are machined smooth for ease in lifting the bayonet tube and placing the bayonet in the combat position.

Receiver

7. The **receiver** (Figure 3) serves to house the bolt assembly. Attached to it are: the feed interrupter-ejector, magazine with follower mechanism, and trigger mechanism.

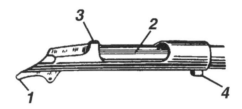

Figure 3. Receiver

1 - tang	2 - upper window
3 - slots for charger clips	4 - receiver lug

Externally, the receiver has:

a) an **upper window** for inserting cartridges and housing the bolt rib. The window has two tapers: the forward taper facilitates the opening of the bolt; the rear portion of the bolt sleeve rib slides along the rear [near vertical] taper as the bolt rib rotates to the right during closing;

b) **grooves** for inserting charger clips with cartridges: one on the right side and two on the left, the forward of which is for the edge of the charger clip;

c) an **upper slot** for guiding the movement of the bolt sleeve rib and hammer;

d) a **tang** with hole for the tang screw and a recess for passage of the hammer's cocking knob and sear lug when the hammer is placed on safe;

e) a **lug** for securing the receiver to the stock; the lug has a threaded hole for the lug screw;

f) a **lower window** for passage of cartridges from the magazine into the receiver and vice versa;

g) a **threaded hole** for the trigger spring screw;

h) **flanges** for the trigger pin;

i) a **slit** for the trigger mechanism with shoulders for the trigger stop during removal of the bolt;

j) and a **slot** for the heel of the feed interrupter-ejector with a threaded hole for its screw.

Internally, the receiver has:

a) a **channel** for housing the bolt assembly;

b) a **threaded well** by which the receiver is screwed onto the barrel tenon;

c) **two longitudinal channels and one circular channel**, into which pass the locking lugs of the bolt head during forward delivery and rotation of the bolt;

d) **slots** [at the front of the receiver on the right side] for passage of the ejector during forward delivery and rotation of the bolt;

e) **tapered ramps** [on the inner sides of the receiver] for guiding the cartridges delivered by the magazine into the chamber;

f) a **projection** on the right side which, along with the feed interrupter-ejector, holds the cartridge just delivered from the magazine in the receiver, preventing it from jumping upward;

g) a **lower channel** for guiding the movement of the connector bar and for passage of the locking lug of the bolt head;

h) and a **recess** on the right side (under the slot for installing charger clips) for passage of the cartridge rims during charging from charger clips.

Feed Interrupter-Ejector

8. The **feed interrupter-ejector** separates the cartridges delivered from the magazine into the receiver and ejects casings (cartridges) pulled from the chamber by the extractor.

The feed interrupter-ejector of the new type (Figure 4) consists of a **feed interrupter** with an interrupting lug and heel and an **ejector** with ejecting lug. The feed interrupter and ejector are joined together by a connecting lug on the ejector that fits into a corresponding hole in the interrupter.

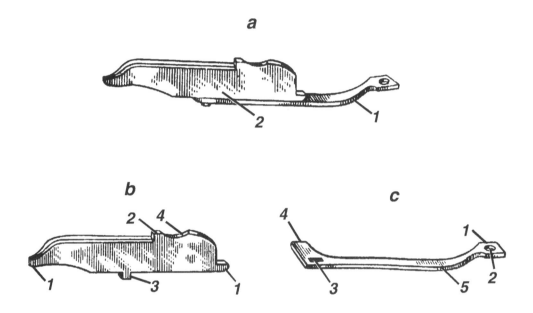

Figure 4. Feed interrupter-ejector of the new type

a. 1 - interrupter   2 - ejector

b. 1 - lugs (protrusions)   2 - ejector lug   3 - connecting lug
       4 - scalloped recess

c. 1 - heel   2 - hole for screw   3 - rectangular hole
       4 - interrupter lug   5 - spring portion

The feed interrupter-ejector of the old type (Figure 5) is a single part. It has a **blade** with ejector lug and interrupter lug and a **spring portion** with heel.

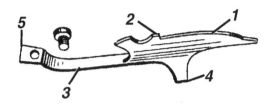

Figure 5. Feed interrupter-ejector of the old type:

1 - blade	2 - ejector lug	3 - spring portion
4 - interrupter lug	5 - heel	

The interrupter (spring portion) fits by its heel in a slot of the receiver and is secured by a screw.

The ejector (blade) fits in a slot in the receiver. Upon opening of the bolt it emerges from the slot into the receiver channel and along with the projection [on the opposite side of the receiver] holds the uppermost (next) cartridge in the receiver channel. The ejector lug fits into a longitudinal channel on the left side of the bolt, and during the rearward movement of the bolt passes through a longitudinal slot on the bolt head and ejects the casing (cartridge) withdrawn from the chamber by the bolt head. The feed interrupter lug fits into a cut-out in the left wall of the magazine. Upon opening of the bolt, it enters the magazine and, pressing on the next cartridge case interrupts (holds) this case from moving upward. On the ejector (blade) at the rear of the ejector lug is a scalloped recess for passage of the cartridge base when cartridges are being inserted into the magazine from a charger clip.

Trigger Mechanism

9. The **trigger mechanism** (Figure 6) consists of the trigger, trigger spring, screw, and pin.

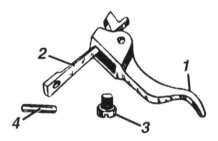

Figure 6. Trigger mechanism

1 - trigger piece	2 - trigger spring
3 - trigger spring screw	4 - pin

The **trigger** serves to depress the sear of the trigger spring during release of the hammer from the cocked position. It has a **finger piece** used by the index finger to release the hammer, a **recess** for passage of the trigger spring, a **hole** for the pin and **bolt stop** which, entering the lower channel of the connecting bar and pressing on its forward wall, stops the bolt during its rearward withdrawal.

The **trigger spring** has a **sear** for holding the hammer at the cocked position and a **heel with hole** for the screw that secures the spring to the receiver.

The **trigger piece pin** passes through the hole in the trigger piece and mounting flanges of the receiver.

Rear and Front Sight

10. The **rear sight** (Figure 7) is used to lay the rifle on the target and to apply the appropriate elevation corrections for firing at various ranges. It consists of the sight base, sight leaf with slider, and springs.

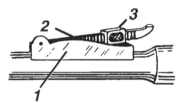

Figure 7. Rear sight

1 - sight base   2 - sight leaf   3 - slider

The **sight base** has two side walls with inclined edges. On the front end of the base are flanges with holes for the sight leaf pin. On the rear end is a slot for securing the sight leaf spring.

The **sight leaf** (Figure 8) is secured by a pin in the flanges of the sight base and can rotate about the pin. At the rear end of the leaf is an **aperture piece** with a notch for aiming.

On the upper surface of the leaf are engraved marks with numbers from 1 to 20. These marks indicate ranges in hundreds of meters, with even numbers on the right side and odd numbers on the left side. Between the marks are inscribed smaller marks for adjusting the sight with a precision of 50 meters.

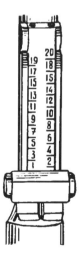

Figure 8. Sight leaf with slider

On the lateral edges of the leaf are notches for engaging in the sight slider.

The **sight slider** fits onto the sight leaf and is held in its adjusted position by catches. Each catch has a spring and a tooth that engages in the notch on the lateral edge of the sight leaf (Figure 9).

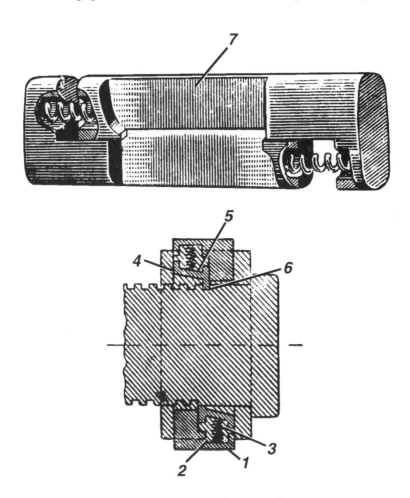

Figure 9. Sight slider catches

1 - detent cap	2 - cylindrical socket	3 - catch spring
4 - catch	5 - socket	6 - lug
7 - recess		

The **sight leaf spring** is secured at its rear end in a slot on the sight base, and by its front end is held by the heel of the sight leaf and itself holds the leaf in the set position.

11. The **front sight post** (Figure 10) is used for aiming. It is secured in a hole in the circular sight cover, which is mounted in a slot on the sight base secured to the barrel (on the Model 1944 carbine– on the fixed barrel tube that mounts the bayonet). A scribe mark is etched on the front surface of the sight guard that is aligned with a mark on the sight base. The front sight guard is secured by staking.

Figure 10. Front sight with guard

1 - sight post   2 - guard

Note: In rifles of early production, the front sight post is inserted directly into a slot on the sight base and secured by staking (Figure 11).

Figure 11. Front sight of early production rifles (with sight guard on bayonet)

Bolt Assembly

12. The **bolt assembly** (Figure 12) serves to deliver the cartridge into the chamber, to close the barrel bore, produce the shot, and extract the casing (cartridge) from the chamber. The bolt assembly consists of the bolt sleeve, bolt head, extractor, hammer, firing pin, main spring, and connecting bar.

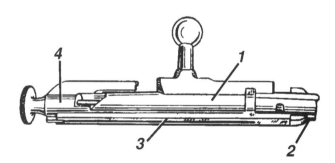

Figure 12. Bolt assembly

1 - bolt sleeve   2 - bolt head
3 - connecting bar   4 - hammer

13. The **bolt sleeve** (Figure 13) has:

a) a **rib** for guiding the bolt's movement in the receiver channel. The ends of the rib have tapers that slide along the corresponding tapers of the upper receiver window: the front taper during opening of the bolt, and the rear taper during closing of the bolt.

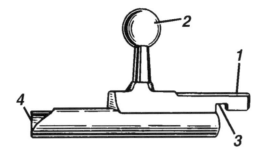

Figure 13. Bolt sleeve

1 - rib   2 - handle
3 - slot for connecting bar retaining lug   4 - spiral recess

b) a **handle** for manipulating the bolt;

c) a **socket** for the bolt head alignment lug;

d) a **slot** for the connecting bar retaining lug;

e) a **tapered channel** for passage of the ejector lug of the feed interrupter-ejector during longitudinal movement of the bolt and for imparting leftward movement to it during bolt closing;

f) a **notch** on the rear face of the bolt sleeve into which enters the tenon of the hammer camming lug and by which the hammer is prevented from rotating during rearward movement of the bolt. [This small notch is immediately to the right of the large camming recess, at about the 5 o'clock position with the bolt handle at 12 o'clock.]

g) a **camming recess**, which during opening rotation of the bolt pushes the hammer with striker to the rear and cocks the hammer;

h) a **cut-out** for the passage of the hammer's safety lug; [The deep portion of this cut-out is at 9 o'clock with the bolt handle at 12 o'clock.]

i) a **small notch** for holding the hammer on safe; [This shallow notch is at 7 o'clock with the bolt handle at 12 o'clock.]

k) a **channel** of two diameters: large diameter for housing the mainspring and connecting bar tube, and small diameter for passage of the firing pin striker. The end of the mainspring, installed on the firing pin, rests at the juncture of these two diameters.

Note. On the sniper rifle the bolt handle is elongated and bent over for ease of action when the scope is installed (Figure 14).

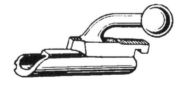

Figure 14. Sniper rifle bolt sleeve

14. The **bolt head** (Figure 15) serves to close the barrel bore. It has:

a) **bolt-head recess with rim** for holding the cartridge base;

b) **two locking lugs** that during bolt closing lie with their rear faces at the walls of the circular slot of the receiver, and during firing withstand the pressure of the propellant gases against the bolt.

c) an **alignment lug** for joining the bolt head with the bolt sleeve. It fits into a slot of the bolt sleeve, enabling the bolt head to rotate along with the sleeve.

d) a **slot** for the retaining lug of the connecting bar;

e) a **slot** for passage of the feed interrupter-ejector during longitudinal movement of the bolt, and also for passage of the retaining lug of the connecting bar;

f) a **slot** for housing the extractor. It has a socket for the extractor heel.

g) a **channel** of two diameters: the smaller for the firing pin striker, and the larger for the front end of the connecting bar tube.

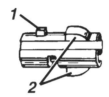

Figure 15. Bolt head

1 - alignment lug   2 - locking lugs

15. The **extractor** (Figure 16) serves to remove the casing (cartridge) from the chamber and to throw it out of the receiver with the help of the ejector lug of the feed interrupter-ejector. It has a **claw**, which engages the rim of the case, and a **heel** for securing the extractor in the bolt head slot.

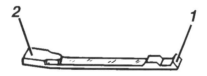

Figure 16. Extractor

1 - claw   2 - heel

16. The **hammer** (Figure 17) serves to cock the firing pin or to place it on safe. It has:

a) a **rib** for guiding the movement of the hammer in the upper slot of the receiver;

b) a **safety lug** (under the rib) for placing the hammer on safe;

c) a **camming lug** for withdrawing the hammer rearward during opening of the bolt. This lug has a tenon for holding the hammer from rotation during the bolt's rearward travel.

d) a **cocking lug** with slots for the connecting bar fork; the sear of the trigger spring catches behind its forward face during bolt closing or rearward travel of the bolt;

e) the **knob** for cocking the hammer (without opening the bolt) or placing it on safe. The knob is knurled for ease in grasping with the fingers. It has a scribe mark on the rear surface for aligning with the screwdriver slot on the rear face of the firing pin.

(f) a **channel**, smooth in its forward segment and threaded in its rear segment for screwing onto the end of the firing pin.

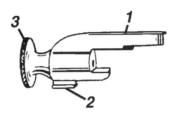

Figure 17. Hammer

1 - rib   2 - cocking lug   3 - knob

17. The **firing pin** (Figure 18) has a **striker** for denting the cartridge primer and a **collar** for a mainspring rest. The collar separates the firing pin into two segments: the forward (short) segment is a **blade** and the rear (long) portion is a **rod** with a threaded end for screwing into the hammer. The threaded end has a **screwdriver slot** for confirming the correct joining of the firing pin with the hammer.

Figure 18. Firing pin

1 - rod   2 - collar
3 - blade   4 - striker

18. The **mainspring** (Figure 19) transmits to the firing pin the rapid movement necessary for the powerful blow of the striker on the primer. It fits on the rod of the firing pin.

Figure 19. Mainspring

19. The **connecting bar** (Figure 20) joins the bolt head with the bolt sleeve and holds the bolt in the receiver during its rearward movement. It has:

a) a **retaining lug**, which fits in a slot of the bolt head and joins the bolt head with the connecting bar;

b) a **stanchion** with rib and tube. The forward segment of the tube fits into the bolt head channel and the rear segment into the channel of the bolt sleeve. Inside the tube is a **channel** for passage of the firing pin. The rear portion of the channel is oval to conform to the shape of the firing pin blade and to prevent its rotation. The stanchion's **rib** fits in a slot of the bolt sleeve and joins the connecting bar to the bolt sleeve. On the left side of the stanchion is a **slot** for passage of the feed interrupter-extractor during longitudinal movement of the bolt.

c) a **fork** into which fit the slots of the hammer's cocking lug;

d) a **channel** (on the lower surface of the connecting bar) for the bolt stop which, contacting the front wall of this channel, holds the rearward drawn bolt from falling out of the receiver;

e) a **taper** (on the upper surface of the connecting bar, left side) for the blade of the feed interrupter-ejector.

Figure 20. Connecting bar

1 - stanchion   2 - retaining lug   3 - fork

Magazine Assembly

20. The **magazine assembly** (Figure 21) holds four cartridges and a follower mechanism. The magazine has side plates, a [front] tang, trigger guard, and a floorplate with follower mechanism.

[Translator's note: While it appears that the magazine holds five cartridges, in fact the fifth (topmost) cartridge is not inside the magazine, but rather in the receiver.]

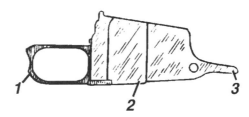

Figure 21. Magazine assembly

1 - trigger guard   2 - side plate   3 - tang

The **side plates** are tightly joined with the tang and trigger guard. The left side plate has a **cut-out** for the ejector lug of the feed interrupter-ejector.

The **tang** has a **lug** by which it fits into the forward portion of the lower receiver window, a **slot** for the floorplate, a **hole** for the barrel lug screw, and a **hole** for the pivot pin.

The **trigger guard** protects the trigger from unintentional engagement. It has a **lug** by which the guard fits in the rear portion of the lower receiver window, a **well** for the latch, a **threaded hole** for the floorplate latch screw, a **notch** for the magazine floorplate, a **slot** for passage of the trigger piece, and a **threaded hole** for the receiver tang mounting bolt.

21. The **magazine floorplate** (Figure 22) closes the bottom of the magazine assembly. A follower

mechanism is attached to it. It has:
   a) a **hook** by which the floorplate is installed on the pivot bolt, which serves as its rotational axis;
   b) a **slot** into which the follower mechanism carrier is inserted;
   c) a **hole** for the carrier pin, which serves as the carrier's rotational axis;
   d) **stops** that limit the upward movement of the carrier;
   e) a **groove** for the carrier spring;
   f) a **threaded hole** for the screw that secures the carrier spring to the floorplate;
   g) a **hole** for passage of the latch;
   h) a round **recess** for the head of the latch;
   i) a **slot** into which the latch lug displaces.

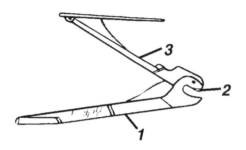

Figure 22. Magazine floorplate with follower mechanism

1 - floorplate   2 - hook   3 - follower mechanism

22. The **magazine floorplate latch** (Figure 23) holds the floorplate closed. It has:
   a) a **heel** with hole for the latch screw that secures the latch to the trigger guard;
   b) a **head** [button] for pressing by the finger to open the floorplate;
   c) a **lug** by which the latch engages the slot of the floorplate.

Figure 23. Magazine floorplate latch

23. The **follower mechanism** (Figure 22) presses the cartridges from the magazine into the receiver.
   It consists of the carrier, carrier spring, carrier spring screw, follower, follower spring, and two pins that serve as axes of rotation.

Stock

24. The **stock** (Figure 24) serves to join together the rifle's components and for ease in using the rifle. The stock consists of the forearm, stock proper, and butt.

The **forearm** has a channel or bed for the barrel with receiver; a **socket** for the stock bolt; a **window** for the magazine assembly; a **slot** for the trigger guard; a **slot** for the sling; and a **cleaning rod path** for the cleaning rod. On the sides of the stock are **recesses** (finger grooves) for ease in grasping the rifle during aiming. On the right side is a **spring** for the barrel bands; on the front end is an **end cap**.

The **butt** has a slot for the sling and a metal buttplate.

Note: The sniper rifle with the faceted forward receiver has longitudinal cutouts on both sides of the upper stock to accommodate the scope mount.

Figure 24. Stock

1 - forearm
2 - stock proper
3 - butt

Upper Handguard

25. The **upper handguard** (Figure 25) with metal end cap protects the hands from burning during firing.

Figure 25. Upper handguard

Bayonet

26. The **bayonet** (Figure 26) is used to defeat the enemy in hand-to-hand combat. It has:

a) a four-sided **blade** [often referred to as "cruciform"] with "valleys" for weight reduction and ribs for strengthening;

b) a **tube** with an elbow-shaped opening for attaching the bayonet to the barrel;

c) a **neck** that joins the blade to the tube;

d) a **catch** with spring for securing the bayonet tube to the barrel.

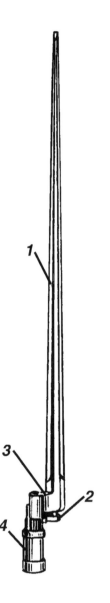

Figure 26. Bayonet for Model 1891/30 rifle

1 - blade
2 - catch
3 - neck
4 - tube

The Model 1944 carbine's bayonet (Figure 27) has a tang with oval hole on its rear end for the attaching bolt, by which it is mounted in the flanges of the non-removable barrel tube. On the rear end of the bayonet is a movable bayonet tube with a self-contained spring. The spring is installed under pressure and strives to move the bayonet tube to the rear. On the lower end of the bayonet tube are [machined] notches for the lower [corresponding] lugs of the flanges. On the front end of the bayonet tube is a bracket with large ring for installation on the muzzle end of the barrel.

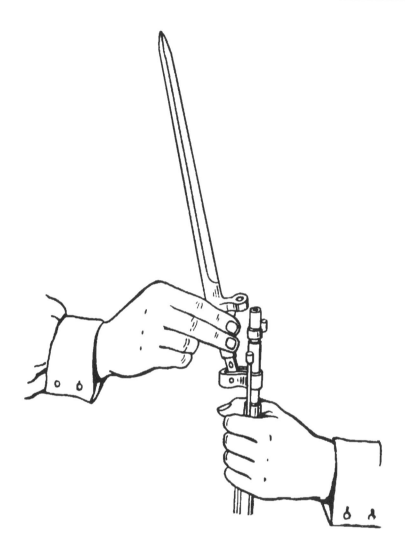

Figure 27. Folding bayonet for the Model 1944 carbine

Note. A portion of the Model 1891/30 rifles were produced with a front sight guard on the bayonet (Figure 28).

Figure 28. Bayonet tube of the Model 1891/30 rifle of early production

Cleaning Rod

27. The **cleaning rod** (Figure 29) is used for cleaning and lubricating the barrel and chamber. It has a **head** with notch and hole for a drift and a **threaded end** for screwing the cleaning rod into its stop in the stock and for attaching the jag.

Figure 29. Cleaning rod

Fasteners

28. The **fasteners** serve to join together and secure the rifle's components. These items include:
   a) two spring-steel, split **barrel bands** (Figure 30);

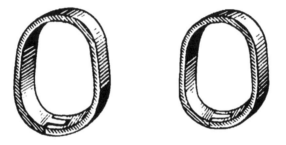

Figure 30. Barrel bands

   b) **barrel band retaining springs**, inserted into the stock to secure the barrel bands (Figure 31);

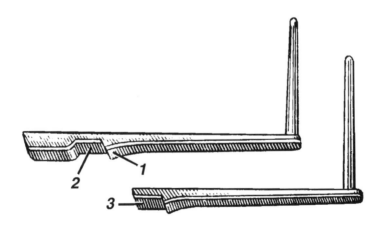

Figure 31. Barrel band retaining springs
1 - thickened segment   2 - notch   3 - ramp

c) **stock eyelets** for the sling mounting slots (Figure 32);

d) **screws–recoil lug** (short) and **tang** (long) (Figure 33) for joining the receiver and magazine with the stock;

e) the **buttplate** (Figure 34) with two wood screws for protection of the butt from damage;

f) **endcap with screw** (Figure 35) to protect the end of the forearm from splitting;

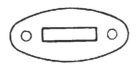

Figure 32. Stock eyelet

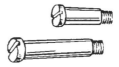

Figure 33. Tang and recoil lug screws

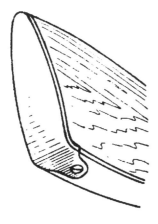

Figure 34. Buttplate

Figure 35. Endcap with screw

g) **stock bolt** (Figure 36) for securing the forearm and recoil lug with the receiver during firing;

h) the **cleaning rod stop** (Figure 37), into which the cleaning rod is screwed for storage.

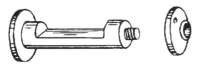

Figure 36. Stock bolt

Figure 37. Cleaning rod stop

Rifle Accessories

29. Each rifle is issued with the following accessories:

a) a **cleaning jag** (Figure 38) for cleaning and lubricating the barrel bore and chamber. The jag consists of a **shank** and a **copper segment** that rotates on the shank.

Figure 38. Cleaning jag

b) a **screwdriver** (Figure 39) for disassembly and assembly of the rifle. It consists of a **blade** and a **handle**. One end of the blade is broad, the other narrow. The lateral edges of the blade have three notches: the middle notch is for confirming the protrusion of the firing pin striker from the bolt head; the outside notches are rested on the bolt head rim during this checking process. One of the outside notches is broadened and is used to rotate the firing pin during the assembly of the bolt and for tightening the jag on the cleaning rod.

Figure 39. Screwdriver with wooden handle

The screwdriver's wooden handle has a metal nut and socket for the blade. In the case of metal combination tools, a case consisting of the muzzle cap and cleaning rod sleeve serves as a handle (Figure 40).

Figure 40. Screwdriver with metal handle

c) a **muzzle cap** (metal or wood) for protecting the barrel bore against damage by the cleaning rod and the muzzle face against damage from the cleaning rod collar during cleaning (Figure 41).

Figure 41. Wood and metal muzzle caps

d) the **cleaning rod collar** facilitates rotation of the cleaning rod during cleaning and lubrication of the barrel bore (Figure 42).

Figure 42. Cleaning rod collar

1 - new type   2 - old type

e) the **drift** provides ease in holding the cleaning rod during cleaning and lubrication of the barrel bore with the wooden muzzle cap; the dowel is inserted through the hole of the collar above the head of the cleaning rod.

f) a **bristle brush**, used for lubricating the barrel bore.

g) a **dual-throated oiler** (Figure 43). The compartment with the letter Щ contains solvent, and the compartment with the letter Н contains rifle lubricant.

Figure 43. Oiler

h) the **sling** is used for carrying the rifle. It has two narrow straps to secure it to the stock.

Notes: 1. Use of other types of accessories is permitted.

2. A single-throated oiler that contains rifle lubricant can be used in place of the two-throated oiler.

Service Cartridges

30. A service cartridge (Figure 44) consists of a casing, primer, projectile, and propellant charge.

Figure 44. Service cartridge

1 - casing	2 - primer
3 - projectile	4 - propellant charge

The casing joins all the components of the cartridge. It has a body, within which is contained the propellant charge, a throat that holds the projectile, and a base with rim for capture of the casing by the extractor claw.

The base of the casing has a **well** for the primer, an **anvil** against which the primer is detonated by the firing pin striker, and **two flash holes** through which the flame from the primer reaches the propellant charge.

The **primer** consists of a brass mantle into which is pressed a **percussive substance**, and a **foil coverlet** that covers the percussive component.

The **propellant charge** of smokeless powder fills the case body.

The **projectile** (type-1908) consists of a jacket and core (lead alloy with antimony), pressed into the jacket. A circular crimp secures the projectile in the case mouth.

The **armor-piercing projectile** consists of a casing and lead jacket enclosing a steel core. The nose portion of this projectile is painted **black**.

The **tracer projectile** consists of a casing enclosing a lead antimony alloy core in front, and in the rear a cup with compressed tracer substance. The tip of this projectile is painted **green**.

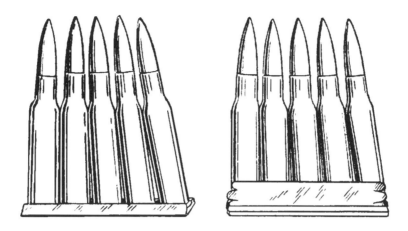

Figure 45. Cartridges in the charger clip

31. The **charger clip** holds five cartridges (Figure 45). It has a channel for the case rim and tabs for holding the cartridges from falling out. Charger clips of the new type hold the cartridges with bent side panels and a spring.

[Translator's note: These clips come from a variety of sources and are manufactured from various metals. Experience has shown that brass charger clips work better than the steel variety.]

Chapter II

FUNCTION OF THE RIFLE'S COMPONENTS AND MECHANISMS

Position of Components and Mechanisms Before Loading

32. The rifle's components and mechanisms are located in the following positions before loading:

    a) the bolt sleeve is in close contact with the lower side wall of the receiver;

    b) the bolt head's locking lugs are in the circular slot of the receiver and are closing the chamber;

    c) the firing pin is released, and its striker protrudes through the hole in the face of the bolt head;

    d) the hammer rib is located in the upper slot of the receiver; the hammer's camming lug is contained in the camming recess of the bolt sleeve. The hammer's cocking lug is contained in the connecting bar fork, above the rear face of the trigger and above the forward face of the trigger spring sear;

    e) the trigger, with its bolt stop, is positioned beneath the hammer's cocking lug; the rear portion of the trigger spring is withdrawn from the lower surface of the receiver;

    f) the feed interrupter-ejector is pushed to the left by the pressure of the tapered slot of the bolt sleeve on the ejector (blade) and is positioned in the receiver wall. The interrupter lug is withdrawn to the left and the spring segment is under greatest tension;

    g) the follower mechanism in the magazine is released and its spring is under least tension.

Function of Components and Mechanisms During Loading

33. To load the rifle, one must:

    1. Rotate the bolt handle to the left.

    2. Withdraw the bolt to the rear to stop.

    3. Insert a charger clip, fill the magazine with cartridges, and discard the charger clip.

    4. Deliver the bolt forward.

    5. Rotate the bolt handle to the right.

    1. **During rotation of the bolt handle to the left:**

    a) the bolt head rotates along with the bolt sleeve because its alignment lug is housed in the slot in the bolt sleeve. During bolt rotation, the locking lugs of the bolt head come out of the circular slots and come into alignment with the longitudinal slots of the receiver. The extractor claw slides along the taper in the barrel tenon.

    b) the bolt sleeve, sliding with its forward taper along the guide of the receiver window, is pushed slightly to the rear.

    c) the hammer, the rib of which is positioned in the upper slot of the receiver, cannot rotate. Therefore, pressure of the camming recess of the bolt sleeve on the hammer camming lug pushes it to the rear along with the firing pin far enough that the camming lug tenon engages in the recess of the bolt sleeve. During this time the firing pin striker is withdrawn back into the bore of the bolt head and the main spring is compressed under the impulse of the firing pin collar, which is withdrawn along with the hammer. The sear of the trigger spring disengages from the hammer's cocking lug and is lifted upward to the stop of the rear end of the spring in the receiver wall.

d) the feed interrupter-ejector protrudes with the ejector (blade) into the deep portion of the tapered slot of the bolt sleeve and under the impulse of the sprung segment is pushed out from the receiver wall. At this time the interrupter lug enters the magazine.

2. **During rearward withdrawal of the bolt** to stop, the bolt stop of the trigger, located in the channel of the connecting bar, stops the movement of the bolt and holds it in the receiver.

3. **During the filling of the magazine with cartridges:**

a) under the pressure of the cartridges, the lug of the feed interrupter-ejector pushes the ejector (blade) into the slot of the receiver and, having allowed passage of the fourth cartridge, rests on this cartridge's upper surface. The fifth cartridge remains in the receiver window and is held on the left side by the ejector (blade of the feed interrupter-ejector), and on the right side by the projection on the wall of the receiver.

b) the follower mechanism is pressed downward, putting the greatest pressure on its spring.

4. **During delivery of the bolt forward:**

a) with the bolt head, the bolt moves the subsequent cartridge into the chamber.

b) the locking lugs of the bolt head enter the longitudinal slots of the receiver.

5. **During rotation of the bolt handle to the right:**

a) the hammer, its cocking lug catching on the sear of the trigger spring, stops and holds the firing pin in the rear position. The remaining components of the bolt continue forward movement as the sleeve, sliding with its rear taper along the taper of the receiver window, is delivered forward.

b) the bolt head is rotated by the rib of the bolt sleeve; its locking lugs enter the circular slot of the receiver. The chamber is reliably closed.

c) the main spring, resting on the collar of the firing pin, is compressed even more.

d) the extractor claw, sliding along the rim of the casing, jumps past the rim and engages it.

e) the feed interrupter-ejector is pressed to the left into the slot in the receiver wall by the tapered slot of the bolt sleeve. The feed interrupter lug frees up the next cartridge. The follower lifts this cartridge up until the uppermost cartridge rests against the connecting bar of the bolt.

Function of Components and Mechanisms During Firing

34. To produce the shot, one must press on the trigger. At this time:

a) the trigger, rotating on its pin, presses with the upper edge of its opening on the trigger spring and causes the sear to be released and to disengage from the hammer's sear lug, releasing the hammer and firing pin.

b) decompressing, the main spring presses on the firing pin collar and delivers it forward with considerable force. The firing pin striker dents the cartridge primer, producing the shot. The camming lug of the hammer enters the camming recess of the bolt sleeve.

Function of the Components and Mechanisms During Reloading

35. To reload the rifle, one must:

a) rotate the bolt handle to the left and withdraw the bolt to the rear to stop;

b) deliver the bolt forward and rotate the handle to the right.

During the rotation of the bolt to the left and its withdrawal to the rear, the components perform the same tasks that were described in paragraphs 33.1 and 33.2, but in addition:

a) the extractor, sliding with its claw along the case rim, pulls the case out of the chamber;

b) during rearward movement of the bolt, the casing, with the left portion of its base coming into contact with the ejector lug of the feed interrupter-ejector, is struck and ejected from the receiver.

c) when the bolt is drawn all the way to the rear, the cartridges in the magazine are pushed upward under the impulse of the follower mechanism. The uppermost cartridge comes into the receiver window and will be held by the ejector (the blade of the feed interrupter-ejector) and the receiver projection. The remaining cartridges are held in the magazine by the interrupter lug.

Function of the Components When the Hammer Is Placed On Safe

36. To place the hammer on safe, draw the hammer knob to the rear to stop and rotate it to the left. During this process:

a) the main spring is compressed;

b) the hammer's cocking lug comes out of the connecting bar fork and enters a recess at the rear of the receiver;

c) the hammer's safety lug enters the small notch of the bolt sleeve and prevents the bolt from opening.

[Translator's note: Some shooters will find the spring pressure on the hammer knob to be exceptionally heavy, requiring considerable rearward pull. This is a normal condition.]

Chapter III

STOPPAGES IN THE NORMAL FUNCTION OF THE RIFLE'S MECHANISMS

General Measures for Prevention and Correction of Stoppages During Firing

37. With proper handling and attentive maintenance and preservation, the rifle is a **reliable and unfailing weapon**.

However, during prolonged combat use, as a consequence of unavoidable wear of components, contamination of mechanisms, or inattentive maintenance, deficiencies might arise in the rifle's mechanisms that disrupt its normal function and cause stoppages in firing.

38. To forestall stoppages during firing, one must:

a) strictly observe the instructions for storage, disassembly, cleaning, assembly, and inspection of the rifle;

b) in winter, lubricate the working components of the rifle with winter rifle lubricant;

c) inspect the charger clip and cartridges before firing; do not load unserviceable and dirty cartridges into the rifle; wipe off cartridges first with a dry rag, and then with a rag lightly wetted with rifle lubricant;

d) carefully protect the rifle against foreign matter (sand, dust, dirt, and so on) during firing, and during rushes and halts.

39. Attempt to correct any stoppage in firing by recharging the rifle, without using excessive efforts. If recharging the rifle does not relieve the stoppage or if the stoppage is repeated, unload the rifle, determine the cause of the stoppage, and correct it.

40. Typical deficiencies that cause stoppages in firing:

Stoppages	Cause of stoppage	Method of correction
1. Magazine floorplate opens by itself: during delivery of cartridges from charger clip into magazine, its floorplate opens and cartridges fall out.	Unserviceable magazine floorplate latch; weak floorplate latch screw; rounded or broken lug.	Load rifle without using charger clip, inserting cartridges into magazine one at a time. Upon completion of firing, having established the cause of the stoppage, correct it or send the rifle to a weapons repair facility for repair.

Stoppages	Cause of stoppage	Method of correction
2. Jamming of subsequent cartridge during delivery into chamber: during its delivery into the chamber by the bolt, a cartridge is jammed by the case rim between the ejector (blade of feed interrupter-ejector) and the right wall of the receiver.	During charging, the cartridge was not placed under the ejector (blade of feed interrupter-ejector); unserviceable feed interrupter-ejector.	Correctly position subsequent cartridge by hand and deliver it into chamber. Upon frequent repeated stoppage, load without charger clip, inserting cartridges into receiver one at a time. Upon completion of firing, send rifle to weapons repair facility for repair.
3. Cartridge fits too tightly into chamber: significant effort required to close bolt.	Unserviceable cartridge; cartridge dented or primer not fully seated; foreign object in chamber.	Remove unserviceable cartridge; if cartridge remains in chamber upon opening of bolt, drive it out through muzzle portion with head of cleaning rod or with jag screwed on cleaning rod, wrapped with rag. Clean and lubricate chamber.
4. Misfire: when trigger is pulled, striker does not dent primer.	Unserviceable primer. Firing pin striker broken or does not protrude sufficiently. Main spring is weak, bent, or broken. Congealed lubricant in channel of bolt sleeve.	Recharge rifle and continue firing; upon frequent, repeated stoppage, remove bolt, check condition and protrusion of firing pin striker and, if necessary, adjust its position. If contamination or congealed lubricant is found, disassemble bolt, wipe dry, and lightly lubricate with rifle lubricant. If firing pin or main spring unserviceable, turn rifle in to weapons repair facility.
5. Case not extracted after firing: upon opening of bolt, extractor claw does not extract case from chamber.	Unserviceable extractor: broken claw or dirt (powder residue, congealed lubricant, and so on) accumulation under extractor.	Remove bolt and confirm condition of extractor. If extractor serviceable, attempt to extract case by energetic opening of bolt. If unsuccessful, drive case out through muzzle with head of cleaning rod or jag screwed on cleaning rod wrapped with patch. Having cleared case, wipe and lubricate chamber. If extractor unserviceable, turn rifle in to weapons repair facility.

Stoppages	Cause of stoppage	Method of correction
6. Case or cartridge not ejected during recharging: upon opening of bolt, lug of feed interrupter-ejector does not eject case (cartridge).	Bent spring portion of feed interrupter-ejector. Obstruction of receiver slot for feed interrupter-ejector.	Eject case by hand (remove cartridge) and clean slot for feed interrupter-ejector. If feed interrupter-ejector unserviceable, turn rifle in to weapons repair facility.
7. Bolt falls out of receiver when drawn to rear: bolt is not retained by bolt stop.	Weakening of trigger spring screw, wear of bolt stop or forward wall of connecting bar.	Having removed bolt, check condition of bolt stop. If serviceable, disassemble rifle and tighten trigger spring screw. If bolt stop unserviceable, turn rifle in to weapons repair facility.

[Translator's note: There are two additional cautions not mentioned in this table that should be addressed. On any occasion that the weapon does not fire after the hammer falls, wait at least 10 seconds before opening the bolt. This will allow sufficient time for a hangfire to go off. If, after firing, you cannot open the bolt (rotate the bolt handle upward and draw it to the rear) with normal effort, ***DO NOT FORCE THE BOLT HANDLE OR STRIKE IT WITH A HAMMER OR OTHER HARD OBJECT***. Your weapon may have a head space problem and should be inspected by a competent gunsmith.]

Chapter IV

INSTRUCTIONS FOR PRESERVATION AND HANDLING OF THE RIFLE

Preserving and Handling the Rifle

41. No matter what the circumstances a soldier might find himself in, he is obligated to keep his rifle clean, handle it with care, and inspect it daily to ensure that it is fully serviceable and **combat ready**.

42. In a barracks and field camp environment, the rifles are stored in racks with open bolts (to relax the sprung segment of the feed interrupter-ejector), with hammers rotated to the left (to relax the tension on the main spring), and with bayonets attached (Model 1944 carbines with bayonets folded).

43. In guardhouse facilities the rifles are to be stored in a rack with open bolts and released hammers.

44. When located in quarters in a built-up area, rifles are stood up or gathered together in a suitable place (away from doors and ovens) with open bolts and released triggers.

45. On the march, carry the rifle on the sling or the shoulder with bayonet attached (Model 1944 carbine with bayonet folded).

At halts, place the rifles in a stack with the use of a cord or place them on the ground with the bolt handle down.

46. During travel by rail, if the train car is not equipped with racks, hold the rifle between the knees with the bayonet removed (Model 1944 carbine with bayonet folded) or place it on the floor so that it cannot fall or be struck. Place the bayonet in a scabbard.

47. During movement by truck, hold the rifle with bayonet removed (Model 1944 carbine with bayonet folded) between the knees, protecting it from being struck.

48. Maintain all the rifle's accessories in clean and serviceable condition.

49. Before departure for exercises or guard duty, inspect the rifle in assembled form and wipe excess lubricant from the exterior metal components. Swab the barrel bore before firing. Protect the rifle against dirt, sand, and dust on exercises. Ensure that the rifle does not fall or is struck by hard objects. Take particular care to protect the barrel and front and rear sights.

50. To prevent occurrences of rupture or bulging of the barrel bore during firing, **never plug the barrel bore**.

51. Before loading the rifle with training cartridges, carefully inspect and wipe them. Do not load the rifle with unserviceable training cartridges.

52. Upon encountering any difficulty in opening the bolt and delivering a cartridge into the chamber, do not use excessive force but determine the cause and correct it.

53. If the enemy employs a droplet-liquid poisonous substance in a combat situation, while covering yourself with your cape or greatcoat, also cover the rifle.

Disassembly and Assembly of the Rifle

54. The rifle is disassembled for cleaning, lubrication, and inspection. Training in disassembly and assembly is conducted only on training rifles.

55. During disassembly and assembly of the rifle, observe the following rules:

1. Conduct disassembly and assembly on a table or bench, and in the field on a clean drop cloth.

2. Handle the rifle's components carefully while removing and installing them, in order to prevent damage.

3. When removing and installing screws, hold the screwdriver with the entire hand and insert the blade tip fully in the screw slot. Loosen screws carefully, taking care not to lift the screwdriver from the screw until it is loose. Then remove the screw by hand.

Use the broad end of the screwdriver to loosen and tighten the tang and trigger spring screws, and the narrow end for all other screws.

4. During assembly of the rifle, pay attention to the numbers stamped on parts so that they do not become intermixed with parts from other rifles.

56. The procedure for partial disassembly of the rifle:

1. **Remove the bolt:** press on the trigger with the index finger of the left hand, and open and remove the bolt with the right hand (Figure 46).

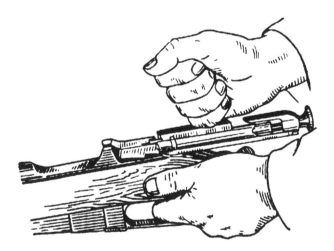

Figure 46. Remove the bolt

2. **Remove the bayonet:** place the rifle with the butt on the ground with the forearm to the left. Grasp the muzzle portion of the barrel in the left hand, and with the thumb of this hand press on the bayonet latch upward to stop. Grasp the bayonet with the right hand and rotate it to the left so that the front sight base is aligned with the slot on the bayonet tube, and then remove the bayonet upward (Figure 47).

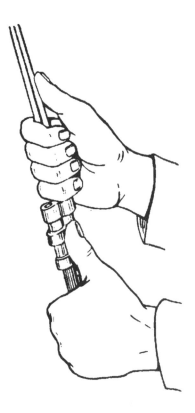

Figure 47. Remove the bayonet

If the bayonet is tight, rotate it with light blows with the palm of the right hand (near the base).

The Model 1944 carbine bayonet folds. The removal and installation of this bayonet is forbidden even during total disassembly of the rifle. The carbine bayonet can be in the travel (folded) or combat (deployed) position.

To place the bayonet in the travel position, place the butt of the carbine on the ground and, holding the rifle with the left hand at the muzzle, with the fingers of the right hand raise the bayonet tube upward far enough so that the ring will pass over the muzzle portion of the barrel (Figure 27). Then, rotating the bayonet on its axis to the left and downward, press its blade toward the stock. During this process the bayonet tube spring presses the tube toward the hinge pin, the tube engages with its lugs on the lower projections of the flanges, thus locking the bayonet in the folded position.

To unfold the bayonet to the combat position, hold the carbine with the left hand just as when folding the bayonet. With the fingers of the right hand draw the bayonet tube downward and then rotate the bayonet on its pin to the right and upward to stop. As the bayonet rotates, it will be lifted upward by the upper lugs of the flanges, and the ring will fit on the muzzle portion of the barrel, locking the bayonet in the deployed position.

Note. Carbines have been issued to the troops without upper lugs on the flanges. To secure the bayonet in the deployed position on these carbines, it is necessary to grasp the bayonet tube and lift the bayonet ring onto the muzzle portion of the barrel and then release it.

3. **Unscrew and remove the cleaning rod.**

4. **Remove the magazine floorplate:** press with the finger on the head of the latch and open the floorplate. Compress the follower mechanism and remove the floorplate from the hinge pin.

5. **Disassemble the bolt:**

a) pick up the bolt in the left hand and, holding the bolt head with the index finger, and the handle with the thumb, with the right hand draw the hammer back so that the tenon of the camming lug comes out of the recess and the cocking lug does not come out of the fork of the connecting bar. Rotate the hammer to the left and release it (Figure 48).

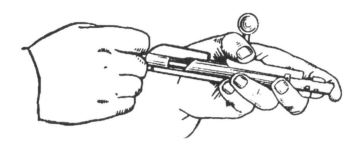

Figure 48. Disassembling the bolt

b) repositioning the bolt in the right hand, with the left hand remove the bolt head with connecting bar from the bolt sleeve by moving them forward.

c) remove the bolt head from the connecting bar.

d) remove the hammer: position the bolt sleeve vertically and rest the firing pin striker on a wood surface. Pressing with the left hand on the bolt sleeve handle, compress the main spring as firmly as possible. With the right hand, unscrew the hammer from the firing pin, gradually weakening pressure on the bolt handle. Remove the firing pin with main spring (Figure 49).

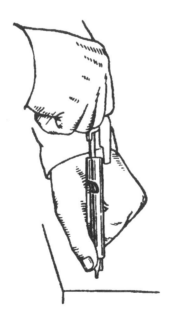

Figure 49. Removing the hammer

e)   remove the main spring from the firing pin.

57. Assemble the bolt:

1. Procedure for assembly of the rifle after partial disassembly:

a) install the main spring on the firing pin.

b) insert the firing pin with main spring into the channel of the bolt sleeve.

c) position the bolt sleeve vertically. Rest the striker on a wood surface and, pressing with the left hand on the bolt sleeve handle, compress the main spring.

d) screw the hammer onto the firing pin and, gradually weakening pressure on the handle, carefully lodge the camming lug of the hammer into the camming recess of the bolt sleeve.

e) using the notch of the screwdriver blade on the firing pin, position the slot on the end of the firing pin in alignment with the scribe mark on the knob of the hammer (Figure 50).

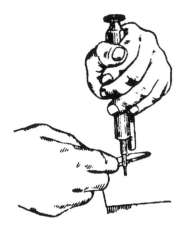

Figure 50. Installing the firing pin

f) with the left hand, install the bolt head on the tube of the connecting bar and rotate it to the right to stop.

g) with the right hand insert the firing pin in the channel of the connecting bar so that its fork engages the slots on the sides of the cocking lug, and the alignment lug of the bolt head fits in the slot of the bolt sleeve. Check the protrusion of the firing pin striker through the bolt head with the notch (or slot) on the screwdriver blade (Figure 51). The striker should protrude to the depth of the middle notch (marked with the number "95") of the screwdriver blade and hang up in the shallow notch (marked "75"). If there is insufficient or excessive protrusion of the firing pin striker, remove the bolt head and connecting bar from the bolt sleeve and screw the firing pin in or out with the appropriate screwdriver blade notch.

Figure 51. Checking the protrusion of the firing pin striker

h) grasp the bolt head with the index and middle fingers of the left hand and the bolt sleeve handle with the thumb. With the right hand pull the hammer back and rotate it to the right so that the hammer camming lug tenon enters the notch on the bolt sleeve. [This positions the rib of the hammer piece in line with the bolt sleeve handle.]

2. **Join the magazine floorplate** with the follower mechanism: press the follower with spring and lever toward the floorplate. Fit the hook onto the hinge pin, release the follower, and close the floorplate.

3. **Insert the cleaning rod** into the cleaning rod well, smoothly release it and screw it to stop.

4. **Attach the bayonet:** position the rifle as instructed in paragraph 56, place the bayonet on the barrel and, pressing downward to stop, rotate the bayonet to the right until it catches.

5. **Install the bolt in the channel of the receiver:** place the rifle on a table with the forearm down and, pressing with the index finger of the left hand on the trigger to release the bolt stop and sear into their recesses, with the right hand insert the bolt in the receiver channel. Deliver the bolt forward, rotate it to the right, and remove your finger from the trigger.

58. Procedure for complete disassembly of the rifle:
  1. **Conduct partial disassembly** (paragraph 56).
  2. **Remove the handguard:**
  a) remove the sling loop from the upper sling slot.
  b) unscrew the recoil lug and tang screws two turns.
  c) slide the barrel bands forward by pressing on their springs (remove the bands in rifles of early production).
  d) remove the handguard.
  3. **Separate the barrel from the stock:**
  a) position the rifle vertically and, holding it firmly with the left hand, unscrew the recoil lug screw (Figure 52).

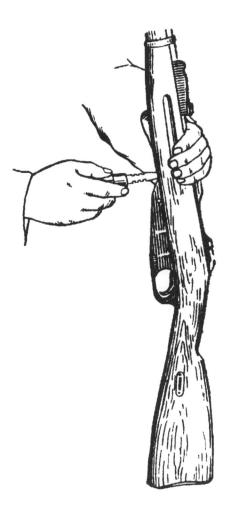

Figure 52. Unscrewing the recoil lug screw

b) place the rifle on a table (bench, and so on), grasp the barrel and magazine in the left hand and unscrew the tang screw (Figure 53).

Figure 53. Unscrewing the tang screw

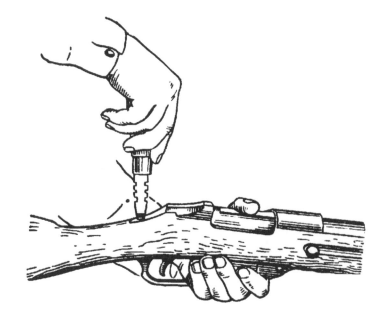

c) remove the magazine.

d) pass the index finger into the receiver channel and separate the barrel from the stock.

4. **Remove the magazine floorplate latch:** unscrew the latch screw and remove it from its well by the head.

5. **Remove and disassemble the trigger mechanism:**

a) turn the barrel over so the rear sight is down and, holding the receiver in the left hand near the feed interrupter-ejector so that the rear sight does not come into contact with a hard surface, unscrew the trigger spring screw (Figure 54).

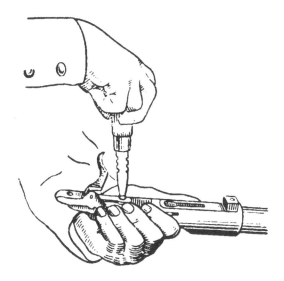

Figure 54. Unscrew the trigger spring screw

b) drive out the trigger pin with a wooden stylus or match stick.

c) remove the trigger with spring from the barrel.

d) remove the trigger spring from the trigger.

6. **Remove the feed interrupter-ejector** (authorized only to supervisory personnel):

a) insert the bolt sleeve in the receiver, deliver it forward and rotate it to the right to dislodge the ejector from its slot in the receiver. Holding the barrel toward you with the left hand and the feed interrupter-ejector facing upward, unscrew the feed interrupter-ejector screw (Figure 55).

b) pressing with the thumb of the right hand on the sprung portion of the feed interrupter along its groove in the direction of the barrel, and lightly lifting it with the index finger of the left hand under by the ejector lug, dislodge the feed interrupter-ejector and then separate the feed interrupter from the ejector.

c) remove the bolt sleeve from the receiver.

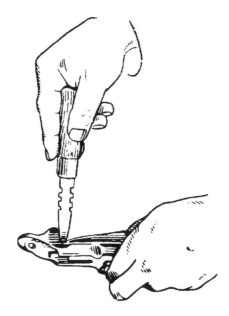

Figure 55. Unscrew the feed interrupter-ejector screw

59. Disassembly and removal of the other components of the rifle can be conducted only in a weapons repair facility.

60. The sequence of assembly of the rifle after its complete disassembly:

1. **Install the feed interrupter-ejector** (authorized only to supervisory personnel):

a) insert the bolt sleeve in the receiver, deliver it forward and rotate it to the right. Position the barrel with the feed interrupter-ejector slot upward.

b) join the ejector with the feed interrupter. Hold the feed interrupter-ejector with the right hand, install the ejector into the slot of the receiver, and the end of the feed interrupter heel in its slot.

c) grasp the receiver with the left hand with the thumb positioned on the sprung portion of the feed interrupter. Rest the thumb of the right hand on the feed interrupter lug. Pressing simultaneously with the left thumb on the sprung portion and with the right thumb on the feed interrupter lug, insert the heel of the feed interrupter in its slot until the hole of its heel is aligned with the hole in the receiver.

d) install and tighten the feed interrupter-ejector screw.

e) remove the bolt sleeve from the receiver.

2. **Assemble the trigger mechanism:**

a) insert the trigger spring in the recess of the trigger piece.

b) place the trigger piece with trigger spring in the small well between the flanges of the receiver and install the pin (Figure 56).

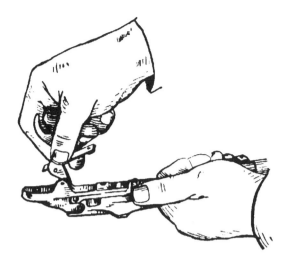

Figure 56. Installing the trigger piece with trigger spring

c) holding the trigger spring with the left hand, install and tighten its screw.

3. **Assemble the magazine with follower mechanism:**

a) holding the magazine with trigger guard toward you, insert the latch in its well with the lug toward the magazine. Holding the latch near the head with your index finger, and with your thumb at the heel, install and tighten the latch screw.

b) join the magazine floorplate with the follower mechanism as instructed in paragraph 57.

4. **Join the barrel and magazine to the stock:**

a) holding the stock with the left hand at the bottom, place the muzzle portion of the barrel into the forearm bed and, guiding the tang of the trigger into its recess, carefully lower the receiver into place.

b) insert the magazine.

c) by turns, in several motions, tighten the recoil lug and tang screws to stop.

5. **Install the handguard:**

a) place the handguard on the barrel and slide it to stop at the rear sight base.

b) install the lower, and then the upper stock bands with split portion toward the cleaning rod. Position them so that the band locks engage.

Note. If the stock has swollen from humidity and the bands do not go into place, leave them where they will find their permanent position on the stock. When the stock has dried out, move the upper ring farther onto the spring.

6. **Assemble the bolt.**

7. **Insert the cleaning rod.**

8. **Attach the bayonet.**

9. **Install the bolt** in the receiver channel.

10. **Attach the sling loops.**

Having completed the assembly, check its correctness and the function of the rifle's mechanisms.

Inspecting the Rifle

61. Periodic inspection of rifles in assembled and disassembled form is conducted by officers and sergeants at intervals established by the Regulation for Internal Service. The inspector determines ahead of time the required degree of disassembly of the rifle.

62. Inspection of the accessories is conducted simultaneously with the inspection of the rifle.

63. The soldier should inspect his rifle daily before departure on exercises and during cleaning. Daily inspection is carried out in assembled form, and during cleaning in disassembled form. Accessories are inspected before each cleaning of the rifle.

64. The soldier is obligated immediately to report to his commander any deficiencies noted during inspection of the rifle and accessories. Deficiencies of the rifle that cannot be corrected by unit resources are to be corrected at a weapons repair facility.

Procedure for Daily Inspection of the Rifle

65. During daily inspection of the rifle, ensure that:
   1) there are no traces of corrosion, dirt, deep scratches, and pitting on the metal components, and cracks or dents on the wooden components;
   2) the bolt, magazine floorplate, and trigger mechanism are serviceable and function properly;
   3) the front and rear sight are serviceable; the front sight stays at an established setting; and the front sight has not moved from the scribe mark on its base;
   4) the barrel bore is not obstructed;
   5) the bayonet is securely mounted (for the Model 1944 carbine, the bayonet tube spring energetically functions and the bayonet freely rotates from the combat position to the travel position and vice versa);
   6) the cleaning rod is screwed all the way in;
   7) the barrel bore is clean (check, if there is any doubt as to its cleanliness).

Inspecting the Rifle in Assembled Form

66. During inspection, ensure that:
   1) the numbers on the bolt, bayonet, buttplate, and magazine floorplate correspond to the [serial] number on the barrel; there are no traces of corrosion, scratches, or pitting on the metal surfaces of the rifle's components and cracks in the stock or handguard;
   2) there is clearance between the receiver tang, its shoulders, and the wood of the stock. This clearance should not be greater than 3.5 millimeters. If there is insufficient clearance, the area of the stock around the tang could become split.
   3) the sleeve rib of the closed bolt does not rest on the wood of the stock;
   4) the bolt does not open when the hammer is placed on safe (check by shaking the bolt handle);
   5) the hammer cocking lug reliably engages the trigger spring sear. To check this, cock the hammer and lightly strike the hammer knob with the palm of the hand. The hammer should not break free.

6) the hammer releases smoothly and the trigger spring sear is sufficiently withdrawn. To check this, press on the hammer knob from above with the thumb of the right hand, and with the index finger on the trigger. The hammer should be released smoothly and the trigger should not touch the trigger guard.

7) the bolt is held by the bolt stop. To check this, open the bolt and draw it to the rear.

8) the follower mechanism, extractor, and feed interrupter-ejector function properly. To check, insert four training cartridges into the magazine and deliver a cartridge into the chamber with the bolt. Close the bolt, open it again, and draw it back sharply. During the delivery of the bolt forward there should be no distortions and hang ups of the cartridges in the chamber, and during bolt opening the cartridges should be freely extracted from the chamber and energetically ejected by the feed interrupter-ejector.

9) the bolt can be freely removed from the receiver. To check this, press the trigger all the way to the rear and remove the bolt.

10) the magazine floorplate latches correctly with the lug of the latch. To check this, open and close the floorplate. Pressing on the closed floorplate upward and downward, ensure that it has only slight looseness.

11) there is clearance between the magazine and the receiver. To check this, release the magazine floorplate and look down through the receiver. The clearance [at the sidewalls] should be within 1 to 2.5 millimeters.

12) the sight leaf is not bent or twisted, does not rattle from side to side, and the line of sight is not disrupted. To check this, press with the fingers on the side of the sight leaf. The sight leaf should return to its place when pressure is released.

13) the sight-leaf spring is securely held in place. To check this, place the slider on 12, then lightly raise up and release the leaf with a finger to ensure that the spring functions energetically.

14) the slider displaces smoothly on the leaf and is held firmly at the markings on the leaf by its catches;

15) the sighting notch has the correct shape and does not show pitting;

16) the bayonet is not bent. To check this, raise the rifle up to eye level and, sighting along the rib of the bayonet, follow its straightness and direction. The line of sight along the bayonet rib toward the buttstock should pass close to the rear sight and small of the stock. Check the rifle with the right side upward. The line of sight across the upper rib of the bayonet should pass approximately along the line of the handguard rib.

17) there is no transverse (90 degrees to barrel axis), longitudinal (parallel to barrel axis), and circular wiggling of the bayonet on the barrel and it is secured reliably by its catch. To check this, lower the rifle with the buttstock down. Place the left thumb on the barrel and ring of the bayonet tube, and with the right hand grasp the bayonet in the middle. Attempt to shake it. The finger of the left hand should not sense any shaking of the bayonet. Rotate the bayonet to the left by its neck to ensure that the catch firmly holds it.

When checking the serviceability of the bayonet on the Model 1944 carbine, keep in mind that insignificant lateral wiggling of the bayonet blade is not a deficiency. Wiggling of up to 2.5 millimeters (measured at the end of the bayonet blade) is permitted in any direction. In addition, the carbine bayonet, thanks to the oval shape of the hole for the tang, must have longitudinal displacement on the pin of 2 to 2.5 millimeters. This longitudinal displacement of the bayonet provides for normal position of the center of gravity of the carbine during firing, eliminating the practical difference of the carbine's zero with the bayonet in the combat and travel positions.

Note. The absence of longitudinal displacement of the bayonet in carbines with a circular mounting hole on the tang of the bayonet involves a change in the normal zero of the carbine when firing with the bayonet in the travel position, as compared to the combat position. The mean point of impact during firing with the bayonet in the travel position is displaced to the left 3 to 3.5 mils from the zero fired with the bayonet in the combat position. [1 mil = 1 millimeter in width at 1 meter of range. This deviation grows to 30 to 35 centimeters (12 to 14 inches) at the specified firing range for confirmation of zero (100 meters). Confirmation of zero is further discussed in Chapter 5.]

18) the bayonet can be removed easily, without excessive effort. For the Model 1944 carbine, check the action of the bayonet tube spring and the reliability of the bayonet locking in the combat and travel positions.

Note. A tight assembly of the bayonet that does not make its removal too difficult is preferable because it ensures reliable mounting of the bayonet.

19) the front sight is not bent and its post is not pitted. It is secured firmly in its base; the scribe mark on the sight base aligns with the mark on the mount. The sight base does not move under finger pressure.

20) the metal at the muzzle of the barrel does not have pits or eruptions and there is no erosion at the muzzle portion of the bore. Rotate the rifle and inspect the barrel bore from the muzzle end.

21) the forearm endcap is firmly attached and does not touch the barrel. The endcap should not rattle and its sides should not touch the barrel surface (check with a piece of paper).

22) the cleaning rod freely screws in and out and is firmly held in its stop. It is not bent.

23) the handguard, stock, forearm, and barrel bands are serviceable. The handguard and forearm should not have cracks or splits that render them ineffective. The stock eyelets should be firmly seated (do not rattle) and the barrel bands should be held by their retaining springs.

Note. The barrel at the muzzle end can have some movement at its juncture with the forearm and handguard, up to 2 millimeters in each direction. But such movement is not required.

24) there are no cracks and splits in the buttstock and the buttplate is securely attached by its wood screws;

25) Inspect the barrel bore and chamber in the light from both ends after swabbing them dry. To conduct this inspection, raise the rifle to eye level and rotate it so that the barrel bore is clearly and then weakly illuminated through its entire length.

During the inspection of the middle portion of the bore, bring the eye as close as possible to the muzzle face and, conversely, during inspection of the more visible portions of the bore move the eye farther away.

The following conditions indicate an unserviceable barrel bore:

Corrosion, observed in the form of dark traces. One can detect corrosion invisible to the eye by wiping the bore with a clean patch on which, in this case, will remain brown spots. A dull surface of the barrel bore that does not leave any traces on a patch is not considered a deficiency.

An **eruption**—the initial deterioration of the bore by corrosion. It is detected in the form of spots or small specks located in specific areas or throughout the barrel bore.

Traces of corrosion, dark shallow spots that remain after removing corrosion.

Cavities, significant eating away of the metal.

Cupro-nickeling, which appears when firing bullets with cupro-nickel cores. It is observed in the form of layers or nodes, and is removed at a weapons repair facility.

Copper fouling, which appears when firing bullets covered with copper and zinc alloy (plated). It is observed in the form of a light copper trace on the surface of the bore and is removed at a weapons repair facility.

Scratches that have the form of lines, sometimes with noticeable raising of the metal at the edges.

Pitting—of greater or less depth, sometimes with the raising of the metal.

Rounding of the edges of the lands, particularly noticeable at the left edges (when viewed from the chamber end).

[Translator's note: The direction of the rifling causes the bullet to rotate in a clockwise manner. This direction of rotation causes the surface of the bullet to make initial contact with the left edge of the rifling, thereby subjecting this edge to greater wear than the right (trailing) edge.]

A **bulge**, observed in the barrel bore in the form of a transverse dark circle, continuous or intermittent.

During inspection of the chamber, ensure its cleanliness and the absence of pitting on the face of the barrel tenon. If any pitting is present, check its influence on a cartridge. Insert an inspection cartridge (without scratches on the surface) into the chamber. Close and then open the bolt. There should not be any scratches on the cartridge.

During the inspection pay special attention to the bores of those rifles in which corrosion and other deficiencies were detected on previous occasions.

67. Completing the inspection of the rifle in assembled form, ensure that the tang and recoil lug screws have been tightened properly. Excessive tightening of the recoil lug screw in itself can lead to loosening of the angle in the joint with the magazine sidewalls, especially if the upper edges of the magazine are in contact with the bottom of the receiver.

68. Upon completion of the inspection of the rifle, inspect the accessories, paying special attention to the serviceability of the cleaning rod, muzzle cap, and cleaning jag. In addition, ensure that all the components of the accessories are on hand.

Inspecting the Rifle in Disassembled Form

69. Inspect each individual component of the disassembled rifle, ensuring that there is no corrosion, dirt, cracks, deterioration of metal, damaged threads, bends, pits, and wire edges.

70. During inspection of the barrel, ensure that:

a) the feed interrupter-ejector is serviceable and its screw is properly tightened. Finger pressure on the ejector should cause it to freely go deeper into the receiver slot, and when pressure is removed it should return to its initial position.

b) the trigger spring screw is properly tightened and the sear is not worn;

c) the locating marks on the barrel and receiver are in alignment.

71. During inspection of the bolt components, ensure that:

a) there is no scoring on the front and rear tapers of the sleeve rib, in the camming recess at the rear of the sleeve, in the recess for passage of the safety lug, and in the small safety notch; the channel through the bolt sleeve is clean; there is no significant fouling on the face of the bolt head; the locking surfaces of the locking lugs are not worn.

b) there are no cracks on the rim of the bolt head and peening on its locking lugs. The extractor claw is serviceable.

c) there is no deterioration or wear of the hammer's safety lug and its camming lug; the cocking lug does not show deterioration or wear; the center hole through the hammer is clean.

d) the firing pin is not bent;

e) the main spring is serviceable—not broken, distorted, or shortened;

f) the connecting bar is not bent, damaged, or cracked, especially at the fork.

72. During inspection of the magazine with follower mechanism, ensure that:

a) there is no peening on the edges of the cut-out for the feed interrupter lug of the feed interrupter-ejector;

b) the latch screw is tightened properly;

c) the lever spring and follower are not bent and they are reliably secured. The lever and follower rotate freely on the pins. With finger pressure on the ends of the corresponding springs, the follower and lever should fall of their own weight. The lever and follower springs function energetically.

d) the follower and lever pins do not move;

e) the magazine floorplate and lever stops are not disfigured;

f) the lever spring screw is properly tightened.

73. During inspection of the stock, ensure that it is not cracked and that the forearm is not distorted; the cleaning rod stop is firmly held in its socket and does not protrude above the surface of the forearm bed; the wells for the tang and recoil lug screws and the threads of these screws are serviceable.

Inspection and Handling of Service Cartridges

74. Upon receiving service cartridges, the rifleman is required to inspect them and to ensure that they are clean and not dented or cracked, and do not have wire edges or traces of green; the primer is not too deeply seated, the projectile does not wiggle nor is it seated too deeply; and the charger clips are clean and serviceable.

75. Having inspected the cartridges and charger clips, the rifleman should wipe them with a rag lightly wetted with rifle lubricant, and place them in his cartridge pouches still in their paper containers. The lids of the paper containers should be open and folded back to the sides of the pouches.

76. The rifleman should handle the cartridges carefully and accurately. **Loss of service cartridges is a criminal offense.**

Cleaning and Lubricating the Rifle

77. The rifle should always be clean and functioning. This is achieved by timely and careful cleaning and lubrication.

78. The cleaning of rifles issued to units should be conducted:

a) if the rifle is not in regular use—not less than once every seven days;

b) after training, guard duty, and non-firing exercises—immediately upon completion of training or exercises;

c) after firing service or dummy [blank] cartridges—immediately upon completion of firing or training. While still at the rifle range (in the field), you should clean out and lubricate the barrel bore and bolt head, and upon return from firing (training) conduct complete cleaning of the rifle. Over the course of the subsequent three or four days, swab the barrel bore with clean patches and, if any residue, corrosion, or blackening is visible on the patch, repeat the cleaning.

d) in a combat situation, on maneuvers, and prolonged field exercises—daily, using breaks in exercises and lulls in battle.

79. Lubrication of the rifle with rifle lubricant is accomplished immediately after its cleaning.

80. Cleaning and lubrication of the rifle with rifle lubricant is carried out by soldiers under the supervision of their squad commander, who is required:

a) to determine the degree of disassembly, cleaning, and lubrication that is required;

b) to ensure that the soldiers have serviceable accessories and good quality materials for cleaning;

c) to ensure that the cleaning is done correctly and completely, after which he authorizes the application of lubricant;

d) to ensure that the lubrication is done correctly, and to give permission for placing the rifle in the rack.

Officers, from platoon commander and above, are required to monitor and supervise disassembly, cleaning, and lubrication of rifles.

81. Cleaning of the rifle in barracks conditions or in a field camp location should be conducted in places especially equipped for weapons cleaning, on tables outfitted or prepared for this purpose, and in a combat or travel situation—on tarpaulins, plywood, and so on, cleaned ahead of time of dust and dirt.

82. Accessories for disassembly and cleaning should be serviceable, and all lubricating and cleaning materials should be clean and of good quality. Lubricating materials should be stored in closed containers with appropriate labels on them, and cleaning rags in special boxes or wrapped in a dense cloth to protect them from dust, dirt, and moisture.

83. The following substances are used for cleaning and lubricating rifles:

a) **solvent**—for removing powder residue and cleaning rifle components (barrel, bolt, receiver, and bayonet) that have been subjected to the effects of propellant gases;

b) **rifle lubricant**—for lubricating rifle components after cleaning;

c) **cannon grease**—for lubricating components of rifles turned in to depots for storage;

d) **winter lubricant No. 21**—a thick lubricant light yellow in color, similar to petroleum jelly—for lubricating all of the rifle's components and mechanisms during the winter;

e) **clean and soft** (well-washed) **rags** or gun-cotton ends—for cleaning, wiping, and lubricating; **oakum**, cleaned of lint—for cleaning only;

f) **bristle brushes**—for lubricating the barrel bore and chamber after cleaning.

The use of other lubricating and cleaning materials is not permitted.

Note. Dehydrated kerosene can be used for thinning and washing lubricant from small and complicated parts. After kerosene has been used, the rifle's components should be carefully dried with oakum, and then with a dry and clean rag.

Inspecting the Serviceability of the Accessories

84. Confirm the serviceability of the accessories in the following procedure:

1. **Inspect the serviceability of the cleaning rod and jag:** unscrew and remove the cleaning rod from the rifle. Screw on the cleaning jag and tighten it with the screwdriver notch, holding the cleaning rod from turning with the drift. Inspect the rod and jag to see that they are not bent. Confirm that the jag is securely attached to the cleaning rod and that its copper segment freely rotates on the steel portion.

2. **Inspect the serviceability of the muzzle cap:** install the muzzle cap on the barrel and confirm that it does not have excessive lateral play on the barrel and will not allow the cleaning rod to touch the walls of the barrel bore during cleaning. To accomplish this, move the muzzle cap to the side and look through its opening. The muzzle face should not be visible. Remove the bolt and inspect from the chamber end. The edges of the hole in the muzzle cap should be aligned with the bore. Check the cleaning jag to ensure that it is not worn. The jag should not fit through the cleaning rod hole in the muzzle cap.

3. **Inspect the serviceability of the screwdriver:** the blade of the screwdriver should not be broken, bent, or chipped. Its blade should fit the screw slots. The notches on the blade for checking firing pin striker protrusion should not be bent. The blade should be secure in the handle.

4. **Inspect the serviceability of the cleaning rod sleeve, drift, and other accessory items** to ensure that they are not cracked or bent.

5. **Inspect the serviceability of the oiler:** it should not be cracked. The caps should have cork gaskets and be screwed on tightly. The lubricant should not leak from the oiler or from one compartment into the other.

Procedure for Cleaning and Lubricating the Rifle and Its Mechanisms

85. The rifle is partially disassembled for cleaning after firing, exercises, training, and guard duty. The rifle is fully disassembled for cleaning if it is extremely dirty or has been subjected to rain (in the water or under snow). In this case:

a) if the rifle has been subjected to rain for a brief time and the wood of the stock and handguard have not begun to swell, the rifle should be fully disassembled, all metal and wood components wiped with dry rags and cleaned out, and metal components lubricated. Upon completion of cleaning the rifle should be assembled.

b) if the rifle was subjected to rain for a prolonged time and the wood of the stock and handguard have swollen, cleaning and lubrication of the rifle should be accomplished without removal of the stock and handguard. Cleaning and lubrication of the rifle should be conducted in dry surroundings (but not near a heat source) so that the wooden components can dry. After the wood is dry, accomplish a complete disassembly and clean and lubricate the rifle again.

86. The procedure for cleaning the rifle:

1. Attach the cleaning rod to the cleaning rod sleeve, insert the cleaning rod through the muzzle cap, and screw on the cleaning jag using the notch of the screwdriver blade. Insert the screwdriver blade into the bore of the cleaning rod sleeve (when using the wooden muzzle cap—insert the drift in the sleeve hole above the head of the cleaning rod).

2. Place a layer of oakum evenly on the ribs of the cleaning jag so that it will pass into the barrel bore with modest effort, filling the grooves. Place the oakum in the form of a figure 8 (the long loops on the copper portion of the jag) with the juncture of the two loops across the end of the jag. Secure the ends (loops) around the ribs of the copper segment of the jag (Figure 57), and wet the oakum with solvent.

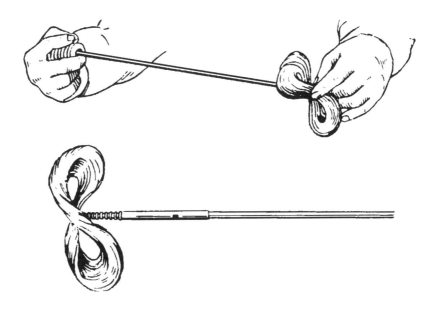

Figure 57. Placing oakum strip on cleaning rod

3. Position the rifle vertically between the knees, insert the cleaning rod into the barrel bore, and move it approximately one-quarter to one-half the length of the barrel. Secure the muzzle cap to the barrel, rotating it so that the front sight is engaged in the circular slot. Leaning the rifle with buttstock forward, place the buttstock on some stable surface. Grasp the rifle with the left hand on the front portion of the barrel near the forearm endcap and smoothly pass the cleaning rod through the entire length of the barrel seven to ten times. Then change the oakum and, wetting it with solvent, repeat this process. Upon completion, carefully wipe the cleaning rod and jag, then swab the barrel bore dry with a clean, dry patch. Inspect the patch. If traces of powder residue or corrosion are visible, swab the barrel bore again with solvent-dipped oakum, and then a dry patch. If the subsequent patch comes out of the barrel bore clean, that is, without blackening from powder residue or the yellowish color of corrosion, remove the muzzle cap and clean the muzzle portion of the bore to the depth of the jag (the installation of the muzzle cap prevents cleaning of this portion of the bore). Then clean the chamber and bullet chamber using the cleaning rod, initially with oakum wetted in solvent, and then with dry oakum and patches.

Having completed the cleaning of the barrel bore and chamber, clean the entire bore once again with a dry, clean patch. Inspect the bore carefully from both ends in the light, slowly rotating the rifle in the hands. Pay special attention to the edges of the lands (for residue remnants).

Notes: 1. A rifle in which powder residue and corrosion cannot be cleaned out in the procedure described above should be turned in to a weapons repair facility.

2. If the cleaning jag with rod becomes stuck in the barrel bore, introduce slightly heated lubricant into the bore and after several minutes attempt to remove the cleaning rod. If the cleaning rod with jag does not come out or the jag comes unscrewed from the rod, turn the rifle in to a weapons repair facility.

Barrel bores that have been damaged by corrosion require especially careful cleaning, because it is difficult to clean the powder residue out of them.

Having ensured the complete cleaning of the barrel bore and chamber, apply an even, modest layer of rifle lubricant on them with a patch. The bore should be lubricated with a bristle brush that has been dipped in the rifle lubricant from the oiler. It is forbidden to leave the bristle brush in the oiler or to leave solvent in a barrel bore.

87. Clean the receiver with the aid of wooden probes and patches dipped in solvent. Clean out slots, grooves, recesses, wells, and holes with a sharpened stick. After cleaning, wipe the receiver dry with a rag and lightly lubricate with rifle lubricant.

Wipe the surfaces of the barrel, rear sight, front sight, and receiver with dry patches and lightly lubricate with rifle lubricant.

88. Clean the bolt in assembled form after guard duty and training without firing, and clean it in disassembled form after firing and field exercises.

Wipe the bolt components with dry patches. Clean the dirt and congealed lubricant out of bores, grooves, slots, and recesses with a wooden stick and patch. Clean powder residue on bolt components with a patch dipped in solvent. Upon completion of cleaning, wipe the bolt components dry and lubricate with rifle lubricant.

Use winter lubricant No. 21 during the winter. Place a thin layer of lubricant on the bolt components.

89. Wipe the inside and outside of the magazine with the aid of a rag wrapped around a stick. Do not remove the magazine floorplate latch for cleaning. Wipe the floorplate with follower mechanism without removing the follower mechanism. Upon completion of cleaning, lubricate the magazine with rifle lubricant.

90. As a rule, clean the trigger mechanism and feed interrupter-ejector without disassembly using dry patches and lubricate with rifle lubricant (with winter lubricant No. 21 during the winter).

91. Wipe the stock, cleaning rod, handguard, all screws, and the accessories with dry patches. Clean out screw slots and recesses with a wooden stylus. After firing wipe the bayonet down with a rag dipped in solvent. Upon completion of cleaning, lubricate the bayonet, cleaning rod, and all screws with rifle lubricant. Do not lubricate the stock and handguard.

92. Excess lubricant can contribute to the rifle becoming dirtier. Therefore, always lubricate components with a thin layer, wiping them with a rag wetted with rifle lubricant. Pass a wetted patch through holes and use a wetted patch over a wooden stylus to lubricate deep recesses, channels, and slots.

Carefully remove the old lubricant during transition from summer to winter lubricant and from winter to summer lubricant.

Use the following guidance for determination of the transition time from one type of lubricant to another. Use rifle lubricant in the summer at temperatures from +50° C [122° F] to +5° C [43° F]. Winter lubricant No. 21 should be used at temperatures from +5° C [43° F] to –40° C [–40° F]. Weapons should be lubricated with winter lubricant No. 21 with 10 to 20 percent kerosene added at lower temperatures.

93. Upon completion of lubrication the rifleman should inspect the rifle in assembled form, and check the correctness of the assembly and function of the rifle's mechanisms. He should finally wipe and pack away the accessories used for cleaning.

Decontaminating the Rifle

94. If the rifle is exposed to chemical agents in combat, the rifleman, using his individual anti-chemical packet, should remove contaminant droplets from the rifle's components that he must touch during the conduct of fire, and then continue the battle.

Complete decontamination of the rifle is carried out after the completion of the battle.

Chapter 5

CONFIRMATION OF THE RIFLE'S ZERO AND BRINGING IT TO A NORMAL ZERO

95. All rifles that are present in units should be brought to a normal zero. Confirmation of zero of rifles is conducted:
   a) upon the issuance of a rifle to a unit;
   b) after replacement of parts or conduct of repairs to a rifle that might affect its zero;
   c) upon detection of an abnormal dispersion of rounds during firing.
   In a combat situation, every commander is obligated to use every opportunity for periodic confirmation of the zero of the rifles assigned to his unit.

96. Confirmation of the zero of rifles is conducted by platoon and company (squadron) commanders. Senior officers, up to brigade-level command, are required to monitor for the careful observation of the regulations for zero confirmation.

97. During the confirmation of zero, firing is conducted by firers selected by the company (squadron) commander from among the best shooters.

98. Before confirmation of zero, the rifles should be carefully inspected and, if required, repaired. A weapons technician or weapons repairman should be present at the confirmation range with a selection of front sights of various sizes and the required tools.

99. Confirmation of zero should be conducted in the presence of the riflemen to whom the rifles are issued, and their squad commanders.

100. Confirmation of the rifle's zero should be conducted in favorable firing conditions (warm and clear weather, calm winds). In the extreme case, it can be conducted in a closed firing range or an area of a range that is sheltered from the wind.

101. Confirmation of a rifle's zero is conducted by firing at 100 meters with the rear sight set at 3. Confirmation of the zero of Model 1944 carbines is conducted with the bayonet in the combat position [deployed]. Firing is conducted with cartridges with the type-1908 projectile from the same factory and lot number.
   A white shield not less than 1 meter in height and 0.5 meters in width with a black rectangle of 30 centimeters height and 20 centimeters width will serve as the target.

102. The point of aim is the bottom center edge of the black rectangle. It should be positioned approximately at eye-level to the firer.

103. The normal position of the mean point of impact is marked along a vertical line above the point of aim with chalk or a colored pencil. With the rear sight set at 3, this point should be 17 centimeters above the aimpoint. The marked point is the control point for determination of the accuracy of a rifle's zero. When firing from the Model 1938 and Model 1944 carbines with the rear sight set at 3, the control point is 19 centimeters above the aimpoint.

104. Firing is conducted from the prone position with a rest. A sack loosely filled with wood shavings may be used for the rest. When firing from the rest, the firer's left hand should lay on the rest, supporting the rifle under the rear sight.

105. To reduce the fatigue factor and improve the firing, firers are permitted to wear a padded jacket or to use a soft pad under the buttplate.

Note. It is permitted to confirm and bring a rifle to a normal zero with a special shooting vise.

106. To confirm the rifle's zero, the shooter fires four consecutive shots, aiming carefully and in the same fashion at the lower edge of the black rectangle.

107. Upon completion of firing the commander inspects the target and determines the accuracy of the rifle's zero by the position of the bullet holes and the location of the mean point of impact.

108. A rifle's zero is recognized as normal if all four bullet holes, or three of them (if the fourth sharply deviates from the other three), **will fit in a circle** (dimension) **of 15 centimeters diameter and if the mean point of impact is not more than 5 centimeters in any direction from the control point.**

Note. For determination of the mean point of impact [MPI] for four bullet holes, connect any two holes with a straight line and divide the distance between the two holes in half. Connect this halfway mark with the third hole and divide the resulting line into three equal segments. Connect the point nearest the first two holes with the fourth bullet hole and divide the resulting line into four equal segments. The point located at the third mark from the fourth bullet hole will be the mean point of impact (Figure 58).

In the event of symmetric location of bullet holes, one can determine the mean point of impact using one of the following methods: a) connect holes that are close to each other in pairs with straight lines. Find the midpoint of the two lines and join with a straight line. Divide this line into two equal segments. The midpoint of this line will be the mean point of impact (Figure 59). b) connect holes that are opposite each other in pairs with straight lines. The intersection of these two lines will be the mean point of impact (Figure 60).

To determine the mean point of impact using three bullet holes, connect two holes with a straight line. Connect the midpoint of this line with the third hole, and divide the resulting line into three equal segments. The point nearest the first line will be the mean point of impact (Figure 61).

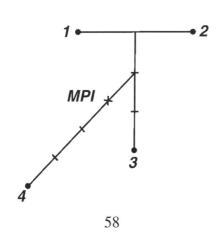

58

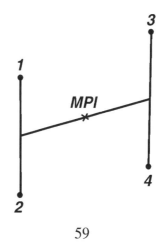

59

52

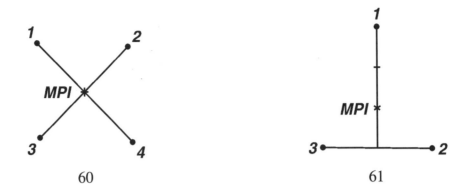

60   61

Figures 58—61. Determination of the mean point of impact with four and three bullet holes

109. If the bullet holes will not fit in the 15-centimeter circle or if the mean point of impact deviates from the control point by more than 10 centimeters, the commander, with the participation of the weapons technician, determines the cause of the dispersion of bullets and their excessive deviation from the control point. After determination of the cause, the rifle is repaired by the weapons technician, at the zeroing range if possible. After repair of the rifle, the firing is repeated. Upon repetition of an unsatisfactory firing result, the rifle is sent to a weapons repair facility. The log book with the results of the first and second firings recorded in it is sent along with the rifle.

110. If the rifle's zero satisfies the requirement for accuracy (bullet holes fit into a dimension of 15 centimeters), but its deviation from the mean point of impact is not excessive (not more than 10 centimeters), then the rifle is given to the weapons technician for appropriate movement, filing, or replacement of the front sight post. The front sight post is replaced with a lower post (or filed down) if the mean point of impact is low [relative to the control point], and with a higher post if the mean point of impact is high. The front sight base (or post) is moved to the left (right) if the rifle fires to the left (right).

Through repositioning the front sight (or post) and repeated confirmation firing, set the front sight (or post) so that the deviation of the mean point of impact from the control point is reduced to not more than 5 centimeters.

111. If the front sight base (or post) is moved or the height of the front sight post is changed, keep in mind that each 0.5 millimeter change in its height shifts the mean point of impact approximately 8 centimeters at 100 meters during firing from the rifle, and 12 centimeters at 100 meters from the carbine.

112. Confirmation of a rifle's zero is considered complete when the rifle satisfies the requirements of normal zero regarding both accuracy for group size and position of the mean point of impact.

113. Upon completion of zero confirmation, the position of the front sight cover (or post) is fixed by the weapons technician, the old scribe mark on the front sight is cleaned off or crossed out, and a new mark is inscribed in its place. It is forbidden to clean the mark from the sight base.

114. The results and time of zero confirmation are recorded in the log book of each rifle and in the individual soldier's firing book. Bullet holes are noted with dots, and the location of the mean point of impact with a cross.

Faults of the Rifle that Disrupt Its Accuracy

115. Typical faults that disrupt the accuracy of the rifle:

a) the **front sight post is bent, broken, or its top is pitted.** The bullets will deviate in the direction opposite the displacement of the top of the front sight post.

b) the **rear sight slider is bent or distorted.** The bullets will deviate in the direction of displacement of the rear sight aperture.

c) the **barrel is touching the side of the forearm end cap.** The bullets will deviate toward the side opposite the contact.

d) the **lands at the muzzle of the barrel are damaged.** The bullets will deviate toward the side opposite the location of the damage.

e) the **recoil lug screw and tang screw are tightened unequally** (too loose or too tight). The bullets will deviate upward or downward.

f) **deterioration** of the barrel bore, especially at the muzzle, **wear** of the lands, **corrosion, pitting, scratches** in the barrel bore, **loose bayonet,** and a **cleaning rod that jiggles during firing** can all cause increased dispersion of bullets.

[Translator's note: The Model-1938 and -1944 carbines are subject to more rapid deterioration of the bore at the muzzle due to the greater amount of unburned propellant that passes this point. Additional care should be shown to cleaning the muzzle portion of the bore, and also to inspecting the bore at the muzzle of these carbines.]

Part Two

METHODS AND INSTRUCTIONS FOR FIRING WITH THE RIFLE

Chapter I

METHODS FOR FIRING THE RIFLE

General Instructions

116. The firing of the rifle is accomplished by the fulfillment of the following tasks: **preparation for firing** (taking up a firing position, loading, and setting the sight), **firing the shot, ceasing fire, and resuming readiness to fire.**

The rifleman conducts fire upon commands of his commander or individually.

117. Firing from the rifle can be accomplished from the prone, kneeling, sitting, and standing (stationary and moving) positions. Firing can be conducted offhand or from a rest.

The rifleman should quickly and automatically accomplish all firing tasks without losing observation of the target, with the exception of the time required to set the rear sight.

118. The command **"Load"** is given for loading of the rifle. Upon this command, the rifleman loads the rifle in the position he was in when the command was issued.

If necessary, a position for firing can be designated before the command **"Load"** is given.

119. The squad (platoon) commander issues a command that specifies the target, sight setting, aimpoint (if required), and type of fire for the opening and conduct of fire.

120. In order to commence firing with a controlled single shot, the commander issues the command: **"Directly at the machine gun, six, at the figure on the left, to the right (left) one at a time—fire"** or **"Reference point 2—white rock, right one finger—infantry in pit, from right to left in sequence—fire."**

When firing in this manner, the rifleman carefully aims and fires the shots in sequence one after another. Fire is conducted until the signal or command is given to cease firing.

121. In order to commence rapid single-shot firing, the commander issues the command, for example: **"At the attacking ranks, three, at the belt—fire."**

The rifleman conducts rapid fire without regard to sequence of targets. The speed of firing is achieved through rapidity in cycling and reloading the rifle, but not at the expense of aiming and squeezing the trigger. Fire is conducted until the command or signal is given to cease fire.

122. In order to commence rapid fire with a specified number of cartridges, the commander issues the command, for example: **"At the enemy group, left of road, four, five rounds at the left figure—fire."** When he has expended the instructed number of cartridges, the rifleman ceases fire.

123. In order to fire in salvoes, the commander issues the command, for example: **"Directly at the column, squad in salvo, five, at the belt. Squad—fire."** Or **"Cavalry from the right—prepare to fire. At the cavalry, platoon in salvo, six, at the horses' chests. Platoon—fire."** Or **"At the diving aircraft, squad in salvo, three, at the nose. Squad—fire."** Or **"At the attacking infantry, platoon in salvo, three, at the belt. Platoon—fire."**

Upon the command "in salvo," the riflemen get ready and load their rifles; upon the command "three" (rear sight setting) they set the rear sight slider. Upon the command "squad" (platoon, company) they take aim at the target, and upon the command "fire" they make the shot, then immediately reload the weapon (in preparation for a subsequent salvo).

To continue firing in salvoes, if the target has not changed, only the command **"Squad** (platoon) **—fire"** is issued.

124. The command **"Cease fire"** is issued or a prolonged whistle is sounded to temporarily cease firing. If necessary, the command **"Hammer"** can also be issued. Upon the first command, the rifleman ceases firing and reloads the rifle's magazine. If the second command is issued, the rifleman places the hammer on safe.

125. The command **"Unload"** is issued for a total cease fire. The rifleman slides the rear sight slider all the way to the rear and unloads the rifle. Then, if firing was being conducted from the prone position, he places the rifle along his body, muzzle portion in left hand to protect the barrel bore, bolt, and magazine from foreign objects. If firing was being conducted from the kneeling or sitting position, the rifleman unloads the rifle, then upon command stands up and places the rifle along his side. If firing was being conducted from the standing position, the rifleman unloads the rifle and individually places it along his side.

126. The rifle can be fired from the left or right shoulder, depending on the physical characteristics of the rifleman.

127. Guided by the basic instructions for preparation for firing laid out below, each rifleman should, depending on his individual peculiarities, develop the most comfortable and reliable position for firing, achieving the same position of the buttstock in the shoulder, the most comfortable position of the body, hands, and feet, and the same position of the elbows on the ground.

Methods for Prone Firing

Preparation for Firing

128. To fire from the prone position, make a full pivot to the right and simultaneously place the right leg forward one-half step. Inclining the rifle with muzzle toward the target, quickly go down on the left knee; then, supported by the left arm, lay down on the left side in the new direction. Place the rifle in the palm of the left hand (under the rear sight) and drop the buttstock to the ground. Shift the right hand to the bolt handle, grasp it with palm down (Figure 62), rotate the handle to the left and draw the bolt rearward to stop. Move the right hand to the cartridge pouch and unclasp and open the cover. Take out a charger clip with cartridges and place it in the slot of the receiver.

Figure 62. Preparing to fire in the prone position

Place the right thumb on the uppermost cartridge near the charger clip (Figure 63) and push the cartridges into the magazine so that the uppermost cartridge is under the ejector (the blade of the feed interrupter-ejector). Remove and discard the charger clip. Placing the soft portion of the palm (next to the thumb) of the right hand on the bolt handle, quickly deliver the bolt forward and rotate the handle to the right to stop.

Note. When loading without a charger clip, insert the cartridges into the upper receiver window one at a time, seating them under the ejector (blade of the feed interrupter-ejector).

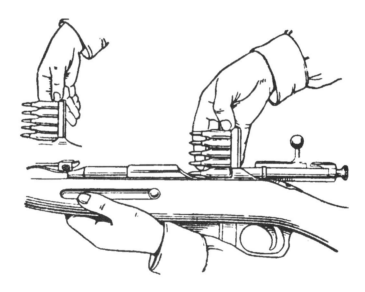

Figure 63. Loading the rifle with a charger clip

Upon completion of loading, lay flat on the ground with legs slightly spread, toes pointed outward, with both elbows on the ground. If you do not expect to commence firing immediately, shift the right hand to the small of the stock. Grasp the stock with the thumb on top and the index finger inside the trigger guard so that it touches the side of the trigger guard. With the remaining fingers, grasp the small of the stock from below tightly, but without tension. Hold the rifle in the left hand with the buttstock resting on the ground and protecting the muzzle from foreign objects (Figure 64).

Figure 64. Position of the rifleman after loading the rifle

129. To set the rear sight at the required marking, move the right hand to the sight and bring the rifle toward your body so that you can better see the required setting. When firing the rifle from the iron sights, press with the thumb and index finger on the slider catches and move the slider so that its front edge is aligned with the appropriate mark on the sight leaf.

When firing the rifle using the scope, remove the dust caps, set the scope at the range to the target, and adjust the windage knob for the required correction.

To set the scope at the range setting, grasp the elevation knob with the thumb and index finger of the right hand and, rotating it in the clockwise direction, place the required scale marking at the index mark.

To set the scope for lateral correction, grasp the windage knob with the thumb and index finger of the left hand and, rotating it, place the required scale marking at the index mark. Use the scale with the + (plus) sign to move the mean point of impact to the right, and use the scale with the – (minus) sign to shift the mean point of impact to the left.

Firing the Shot

130. Firing the shot consists of shouldering the rifle, taking aim, and squeezing the trigger.

131. To shoulder the rifle, tightly insert the buttstock into the shoulder without losing sight of the target. Simultaneously lean the head slightly forward and, without tensing or extending the jaw, touch the right cheek to the stock. Support the rifle on the palm (close to the thumb) at the stock handholds or at the magazine with the left hand under the rifle's forearm. Grasp the small of the stock with the relaxed right hand and place the index finger on the trigger up to the first joint (Figure 65).

Figure 65. Position for firing with iron sights

132. During aiming, hold your breath at a natural exhale, squint the left eye, and with the right eye look across the rear sight aperture at the front sight post. The front sight post should be in the middle of the notch and the top of the front sight post should be level with the upper edges of the rear aperture (Figure 66). With the sights in this position, bring the rifle to the aimpoint, simultaneously squeezing the trigger.

Figure 66. Level sight picture when aiming with open sights

Note. If it is difficult for the rifleman to close one eye separately, it is permitted to aim with both eyes open. But aiming must be conducted with only one eye, while the other eye is directed straight at the target.

When aiming with the scope, the eye is positioned approximately 8 centimeters from the ocular lens on the longitudinal axis of the scope. Place the vertical post under the aimpoint. The lateral leveling hairs should be positioned horizontally and the rifleman should see the scope's entire field of view (Figure 67).

Figure 67. Aiming with the scope

133. To release the hammer, holding your breath, smoothly squeeze the trigger with the first joint of the index finger until the hammer, unnoticed to the firer, as if by itself, is released from the sear, firing the shot. During the squeezing of the trigger, the pressure on the trigger should be straight to the rear. The rifleman should gradually increase the pressure on the trigger at those moments when the top of the leveled front sight post coincides with the aimpoint. When the front sight deviates from the aimpoint, the rifleman should, without increasing or decreasing pressure on the trigger, correct the lay and, as soon as the leveled front sight is on the target, renew pressure on the trigger. During the release of the hammer, do not be disturbed by a small movement of the leveled front sight from the aimpoint. An effort to pull the trigger at the exact moment of greatest coincidence of the front sight with the aimpoint in itself leads to jerking the trigger, and hence an imprecise shot. If the rifleman, while squeezing on the trigger, feels that he cannot hold his breath any longer, he must, without increasing or decreasing pressure on the trigger, take another breath and, holding it again, continue to squeeze the trigger.

Each rifleman should be able to release the hammer smoothly in 1 to 2 seconds in order to be able to fire 10 aimed shots in one minute.

Reloading

134. Having released the hammer, immediately reload the rifle. Grasp the rifle in the position for reloading, open the bolt to eject the fired casing (cartridge), and close it again to deliver a new cartridge into the chamber.

To preserve the uniform lay and speed up firing at the same target, the rifleman can reload the rifle without removing the stock from his shoulder. Holding the rifle in the shoulder with the left hand, use the fingers of the right hand to cock the hammer; then reload the rifle.

Ceasing Fire and Reestablishing Readiness to Fire

135. A cease-fire can be temporary or total. In the first case place the hammer on safe, and in the second unload the rifle.

136. To place the hammer on safe, draw the rear sight slider all the way to the rear, open the bolt, catch the cartridge extracted from the chamber, and close the bolt to recharge the rifle. Secure the buttplate in the bend of the right elbow or press the stock into the chest with this elbow, whichever is more comfortable. Grasp the hammer by its knob with the fingers of the right hand and rotate it to the left. Check to ensure that the bolt does not open (shake the bolt handle).

137. To renew firing if the hammer was placed on safe, grasp the rifle in the position for reloading, position the buttstock as instructed in paragraph 136, draw the hammer knob to the rear, and rotate it to the right. Carefully cock the hammer; adjust the rear sight, and move the hand to the small of the stock.

138. For a total cease-fire, slide the rear sight slider all the way to the rear; open the bolt to extract the casing, and if there was an unfired cartridge in the chamber, catch it and place it in the cartridge pouch. With the right thumb, push the uppermost cartridge in the magazine under the lug of the feed interrupter-ejector. With the right index finger press the magazine floorplate latch toward the trigger guard, open it with the thumb and middle fingers and, catching the falling cartridges in the palm, place them in the pouch. Close the magazine floorplate and smoothly release the hammer, holding it with the thumb on the knob so that it does not jump. Close the cover on the cartridge pouch and fasten it.

Methods for Firing from the Kneeling Position

139. To fire from the kneeling position, grasp the rifle with the left hand under the rear sight with the muzzle toward the target. Simultaneously planting the right foot to the rear, quickly drop down on the right knee and sit back on the heel. Place the left arm on the upper left thigh and move the right hand to the bolt handle. Load the rifle and adjust the sight as instructed in paragraph 129. Hold the left shin as vertical as possible. The upper left and right legs should form an angle slightly less than 90° (Figure 68).

Figure 68. Preparing to fire from the kneeling position

140. To lay the rifle from the kneeling position, place the left elbow on the soft portion of the leg or, depending on the body position, somewhat in front of the knee. Bring the right elbow up and place the rifle's buttstock into the shoulder (Figure 69). Aiming, firing the shot, reloading, and ceasing fire are conducted in the same manner as in the prone position.

Figure 69. Firing from the kneeling position

Methods for Firing from the Sitting Position

141. One of the following methods can be used for firing from the sitting position:

a) sit on the ground at a 90° angle in relation to the target and firmly dig the heels into the ground. Place the left arm on the upper left leg in a comfortable spot, and grasp the rifle in this hand under the rear sight. Open the bolt with the right hand, load the rifle, and set the rear sight in the same manner as when firing in the prone position.

b) cross your legs and place them underneath you so that the right foot will fit between the upper and lower left leg or so that the left foot will be pressed under the shin of the right leg. Place the left arm on the upper left leg in a comfortable spot, and grasp the rifle in this hand under the rear sight. Open the bolt with the right hand, load the rifle, and set the rear sight in the same manner as when firing in the prone position.

When laying the rifle in the sitting position, rest both elbows on the knees or, if the rifleman's anatomy permits, rest them behind the knees (Figures 70–71).

Figures 70–71. Laying the rifle while in the sitting position

The remaining aspects of firing the shot and ceasing fire are accomplished in the same manner as when firing from the prone position.

Methods for Firing from the Standing Position

142. To fire from the standing position, turn 90° to the right in relation to the target and, without moving the left leg forward, extend it to the left about a shoulder's width. Distribute the body's weight equally on both legs. Simultaneously extend the rifle with the muzzle toward the target with the right hand and grasp it with the left hand under the rear sight. Press the left elbow into the side; move the right hand to the bolt, load the rifle, and set the rear sight in the same manner as when firing in the prone position (Figure 72).

Figure 72. Preparing for firing from the standing position

To lay the rifle in the standing position, place the rifle's magazine on the palm of the left hand, close to the soft base of the thumb. Place the buttstock into the shoulder and press the left elbow into the side or place it on the cover of the cartridge pouch. Hold the right elbow at or slightly below shoulder level (Figure 73). The remaining aspects of firing the shot and ceasing fire are accomplished in the same manner as when firing in the prone position.

Figure 73. Laying the rifle for firing from the standing position

Methods for Firing from a Rest or Support

143. The use of a support significantly eases firing conditions, permits camouflage and concealment, and creates for the rifleman a cover against enemy observation and fire.

The support should provide the rifleman with a comfortable firing position.

To fire from a support, place the rifle's forearm (under the stock bolt) directly on the support, holding the buttstock downward with the left hand near the right shoulder (Figure 74).

Figure 74. Firing from a support

Cover a hard support with a folded greatcoat, sod, and so on.

When firing from a support, it is permitted to position the rifle not on the support, but on the palm of the left hand, which is placed on the support.

Methods for Firing from Behind Cover

144. When firing from behind cover from the kneeling or standing position, lean with the left side and shoulder tightly into the cover, taking care that the rifle and the left hand supporting it do not touch the support. This will prevent the bullets from deviating to the side (Figure 75).

Figure 75. Firing from behind a tree

Methods for Firing from Skis

145. To fire on skis in the prone position, grasp the rifle in the right hand with the ski poles in the left. Leaving the heels of the skis in place, spread the points to the side. Leaning on the poles, go down first on the left, and then on the right knee. Quickly lie down, placing the poles on the snow in front of you. Place the left elbow on the poles and grasp the rifle in both hands (Figure 76).

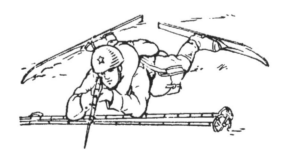

Figure 76. Preparing to fire on skis in the prone position

To fire on skis in the kneeling position, place the poles on the left side. Turn the point of the right ski to the right and place its rear end on the heel of the left ski. Drop the right knee down onto the right ski and grasp the rifle (Figure 77).

Figure 77. Preparing to fire on skis in the kneeling position

To fire on skis in the standing position, take up a position in the same manner as for firing without skis (Figure 78). You can use the ski poles as a rest for greater stability in firing from the standing position. Fasten the poles together and hang them on your left arm by the straps (Figure 79). Place the poles on the left side and rest the rifle on them.

Figure 78. Firing on skis in the standing position

Figure 79. Firing on skis in the standing position using a support

Methods for Firing from Horseback

146. To prepare for firing from a horse, hold the reins in the left hand, drop the right hand between the sling and the buttstock, and bring the rifle to the right and forward with the right arm. Grasp the rifle at the small of the stock with the right hand. Holding the rifle in the right hand so that the muzzle is to the left of the horse's head, and supporting the rifle with the left hand, cock the bolt, charge the rifle (if the chamber was empty), and set the sight.

To fire in a stationary mode, position the horse at 90° to the right in relation to the target so that the direction of firing passes off the horse's left shoulder.

Lean the body slightly forward at the moment of firing, pressing tightly with the knees on the saddle and turning the toes slightly inward.

To fire while the horse is moving forward, lightly raise up in the stirrups, lean the body forward, and increase the pressure on the knees. Hold the rifle over the horse's head.

To fire to the side from the direction of movement, slightly raise up in the stirrups, turn the body toward the target, and lean forward. Increase the pressure on the right (left) stirrup.

To fire downward, slightly raise up in the stirrups and lean the body as far forward and downward as possible, increasing the pressure on the right (left) stirrup.

Chapter II

REGULATIONS FOR THE CONDUCT OF FIRE FROM THE RIFLE IN COMBAT

General Instructions

147. As a rule, the rifleman conducts fire in combat as a member of his squad upon command of the squad commander or by himself, depending on the situation.

148. Fire from the rifle and carbine is characterized by the following data:

Range in meters	Maximum magnitude of mean trajectory over line of sight in cm		Sizes of effective zones of fire in centimeters			
	rifle	carbine	rifle	carbine	rifle	carbine
100	3	2	7	8	6	8
200	7	8	13	14	11	13
300	20	23	19	21	17	19
400	40	45	26	29	24	26
500	70	90	34	39	32	34
600	120	140	43	51	41	43
700	180	210	53	65	51	54
800	270	310	65	81	62	67

The number of cartridges required for reliable defeat of single exposed targets is shown in the following table:

Firing range in meters	head	chest	running	full height	light machine gun
100	1 (1)	1 (1)	1 (1)	1 (1)	1 (1)
200	1 (2)	1 (1)	1 (1)	1 (1)	1 (1)
300	2 (3)	1 (2)	1 (1)	1 (1)	1 (1)
400	2 (4)	2 (3)	2 (2)	2 (2)	2 (2)
500	3 (5)	2 (3)	2 (3)	2 (2)	2 (2)
600	4 (6)	3 (4)	3 (3)	2 (3)	2 (3)
700	5 (9)	3 (6)	3 (4)	2 (4)	2 (3)
800	7 (12)	4 (8)	4 (5)	3 (6)	3 (4)

Notes: 1. The mean point of impact coincides with the middle of the target.
2. The number of cartridges required for the carbine is shown in parentheses.

Selection of Site and Position for Firing

149. The site for firing should be suitable, ensure good fields of fire, and cover the rifleman from enemy observation and fire.

150. Having occupied a site for firing, the rifleman should dig in and construct a support for his rifle.

151. The most suitable position for firing in combat is the prone position. It is the least tiring, ensures the best accuracy, covers the rifleman from enemy observation and fire, and facilitates the seeking and construction of a support and cover.

152. The kneeling or standing position is employed in combat in those cases when the prone position does not provide visibility. These positions can be used when firing from a trench, a fold in the terrain, in grass, light bushes, and from behind cover (corner of a building, tree, fence, and so on), and also in the event of an unanticipated encounter with the enemy, when there is not time to assume a prone position. The standing position is also used for taking snap shots during movement in the attack, from halts of 1 to 2 seconds for firing the shot. In the presence of suitable cover (ditch, shell crater), the sitting position can also be used in combat.

Observation of the Battlefield

153. The rifleman should attentively and continuously monitor the battlefield for timely detection of targets, paying special attention to approaches from the enemy side and places suitable for firing assets and observation points. During observation, do not omit anything from the field of view, because the most insignificant signs and phenomena (shaking of leaves, bushes, movement of grass, appearance of new small objects, change in position and form of local objects, flash of metallic parts and glass, muzzle flashes, smoke, dust, and so on) can facilitate for the rifleman the exposure of the enemy. It is also necessary to listen attentively to sounds of firing and determine the location of the enemy firing position by these sounds.

154. The rifleman should report immediately to his nearest commander anything noted on the battlefield. The report should be brief and precise, for example: **"Straight ahead, yellow bush, close right—machinegun,"** or **"Reference point 3, two fingers right, under bush—observer."**

Target Selection

155. Enemy commanders and individual solders located in the open or half-covered, suddenly appearing or running are appropriate targets for the rifleman in combat.

156. If the commander assigns a target to a rifleman, the rifleman should quickly identify and destroy the target.

During the shooting of a group target, the rifleman should conduct fire directly in front of himself, coordinating his fire with that of his neighbors in order that there not be any unserviced sectors or excessive concentration of fire on one sector of the target.

157. During the individual conduct of fire, the rifleman should be guided in target selection by the target's combat significance, firing first at important and dangerous targets. Examples are enemy firing assets, command personnel, observers, runners, ammunition bearers, leading soldiers, and so on. When targets are of equal value, select the nearest and most vulnerable first.

If during firing a new, more important or dangerous target should appear, the rifleman should quickly shift fire to the new target.

Determination of Range to Targets in Combat

158. The most important factor for the successful conduct of fire is a precise determination of the range to the target.

The precision of the range determination should be greater as the range itself increases.

159. The rifleman's basic means of determining range to the target in combat is visual determination.

In addition, the rifleman should be able to measure range directly by pacing off terrain and by the angles of magnitude with the help of the mil formula.

Visual Determination of Range

160. The determination of range by eye can be accomplished **by degree of visibility of objects or targets** to which the range has been determined, **by sectors of terrain** that are firmly established in the rifleman's memory, or by means of combining one or another methods.

161. To determine the range **by degree of visibility of objects or targets**, each rifleman should have his own (individual) memory aid (table) in which should be indicated how he sees various objects and targets at various ranges.

Below is presented a sample memory aid (table) for normal vision and favorable conditions of range determination (good weather, bright illumination, and so on).

Range in meters	What is visible
1000	Infantryman barely distinguishable from horse rider
800 – 700	Leg movement of walking or running infantryman is noticeable
400 – 300	Patches of color visible on human figure
200	Head and shoulder features of person distinguishable
150	Hands, details of weapon and clothing can be seen

A similar memory aid should be assembled by riflemen for various targets and local objects for the determination of range in both good and bad weather conditions.

When measuring range, keep in mind that the precision of the determination of range depends on the visual acuity of the riflemen, and also on the sizes and clarity of the features of objects, their color relative to the surrounding background, the illumination level, air transparency, and so on.

Here are some examples:

a) small objects (bushes, rocks, individual soldier figures) seem farther away than larger objects (forest, mountain, village, column) located at the same distance from the observer;

b) bright-colored (white, orange) objects seem closer than dark-colored (blue, black, brown) objects;

c) a monochromatic, monotonous background (meadow, snow, plowed field) separates out and seemingly brings objects that are located on them closer if they are of a different color; conversely, if the background is variegated or multi-colored, it camouflages the objects and makes them seem farther away.

d) on an overcast day, in rain, dusk, fog, and so on, all ranges seem increased, and on a bright sunny day, conversely, ranges seem reduced;

e) all visible objects appear to be closer in mountainous terrain;

Taking all these peculiarities into account, the rifleman should be able to make appropriate corrections during the determination of range.

162. The measurement of range **by segments of terrain** established in the memory of the rifleman is suitable only on more or less flat terrain. Any normal distance with which the rifleman is familiar and which therefore is firmly entrenched in his visible memory, segments of 100, 200, or 400 meters, can be used as this distance.

This segment must be mentally (by eye) overlaid in depth as many times as it can be placed. Consider the following during this process:

a) that with an increase in range the apparent magnitude of the segment is gradually reduced in perspective;

b) that hollows (ravines, depressions, streams, and so on) that intersect the terrain under observation, if they are not seen or only partially seen by the observer, conceal the distance.

163. The following methods are recommended for refining and facilitating for the observer the determination of range:

a) the comparison of a specific distance with another, earlier known or measured, though it might lie in another direction; for example, with the measured range to determined reference points;

b) mental dividing up of the distance into several equal segments so that it is possible to determine more precisely the extent of one of them, and then multiply that magnitude by the number of segments;

c) the determination of range by several riflemen and then a calculation of the average. For example, the range estimated by one rifleman is 700 meters and by another is 600 meters. The average would be $(700 + 600) \div 2 = 650$ meters.

164. The habit of rapid and precise range determination by eye can be acquired only as a result of persistent and constant training. It is a goal toward which every rifleman should strive, using every suitable opportunity.

Determining Range by Direct Measurement of Terrain

165. When determining the range by direct measurement of terrain, count paces in pairs when the left or right foot strikes the ground. The soldier must have determined ahead of time the average magnitude of one pair of his steps. For this purpose, measure out (with a tape measure or meter stick) on flat terrain a distance of not less than 200 meters. Walk this distance 2–3 times, each time counting pairs of steps. For example, three passes at the 200-meter course yielded results of 130, 131, and 129 pairs of steps. The average magnitude of one pair of steps is equal to:

$$(130 + 131 + 129) \div 3 = 130;$$
$$200 \div 130 = 1.54 \text{ meters}$$

Example. Measurement of the distance resulted in 260 pairs of steps. The distance (range) is thus equal to $260 \times 1.54\text{m} = 400$ meters.

Determining Range by Angular Magnitude of Local Objects

166. For determination of range by this method, it is necessary to know the precise width or height of an object (target) to which the range is being determined, to measure the angular magnitude of this object (target) in mils, and then compute the range using the formula:

$$R = (W \times 1000) \div M$$

where R is the range, W is the width (or height) of the object in meters, and M is the angular magnitude of the object in mils.

To measure the angular magnitude of an object, one can use a millimeter scale of a ruler, a binocular reticule, fingers (width), and various small objects in the possession of a rifleman, the angular magnitude of which is known to him.

Examples. A tree is 20 meters tall and is covered by two large marks in a binocular reticule. The range to the tree is 1000 meters.

[Translator's note. Each mark in the binocular reticule is 10 mils.]

$$R = (20 \text{ meters} \times 1000) \div 20 = 1000 \text{ meters}$$

A fence that extends for 21 meters is covered by the thickness of a match box (30 mils). The range to the fence is 700 meters.

$$R = (21 \text{ meters} \times 1000) \div 30 = 700 \text{ meters}$$

Sight Setting and Aimpoint Selection

167. During the selection of the rear sight setting, be guided first of all by the range to the target.

168. The aimpoint, as a rule, is the middle lower edge of the target.

When firing at tall targets (running figures and so on) at close ranges, select an aimpoint on the broad portion of the target (chest, waist).

While firing pay attention to the ricochet of bullets and, if necessary, change the aimpoint.

169. When firing from the rifle at ranges up to 500 meters, the temperature and longitudinal wind [headwind or tailwind] render insignificant influence on the flight of the bullet and therefore do not have to be considered in selecting the sight setting and aimpoint.

When firing at ranges greater than 500 meters, the influence of temperature and longitudinal wind must be considered in shifting the aimpoint. Raise the point of aim when firing in cold weather or in strong headwind conditions, and lower the point of aim when firing in hot weather or strong tailwind conditions, guided by the data in the following table:

Firing range in meters

Firing range in meters	Temperature in degrees Centigrade									In strong (8m/sec) tailwind, lower aimpoint; in headwind, raise aimpoint (in cm)
	+45	+35	+25	+15	+5	–5	–15	–25	–35	
	lower aimpoint				raise aimpoint					
	in centimeters									
100	1	1	-	-	-	1	1	2	2	-
200	3	2	1	-	1	2	3	4	5	-
300	6	4	2	-	2	4	6	8	10	-
400	12	8	4	-	4	8	12	16	20	1
500	21	14	7	-	7	14	21	28	35	2
600	36	24	12	-	12	24	36	48	60	3
700	63	42	21	-	21	42	63	84	105	6
800	105	70	35	-	35	70	105	140	175	12

[Translator's note: To convert C° to F°, multiple the Centigrade temperature by 9/5 and add 32°. The converted temperatures in this chart are, from left to right: 113, 95, 77, 59, 41, 23, 5, –13, and –31.]

When firing at ranges of 500 meters and greater, corrections for the influence of temperature can also be made in rear sight settings, guided by the following table:

Firing range in meters	Temperature in degrees Centigrade								
	+45	+35	+25	+15	+5	–5	–15	–25	–35
	reduce sight setting			increase sight setting					
	in rear sight markings								
500	1/2	-	-	-	-	-	1/2	1/2	1/2
600	1/2	-	-	-	-	-	1/2	1/2	1/2
700	1/2	1/2	-	-	-	1/2	1/2	1/2	1
800	1/2	1/2	-	-	-	1/2	1/2	1	1

[Translator's note: To convert C° to F°, multiple the Centigrade temperature by 9/5 and add 32°. The converted temperatures in this chart are, from left to right: 113, 95, 77, 59, 41, 23, 5, –13, and –31.]

170. A crosswind exerts a significant influence on the flight of the bullet, pushing it to the side. Therefore, it is necessary to shift the aimpoint in the direction from which the wind is blowing, using the following table:

Firing range in meters	Moderate wind (4 meters per second) 90°		Moderate wind (4 meters per second) 45°	
	displacement of aimpoint			
	in centimeters	in human forms	in centimeters	in human forms
100	3	-	2	-
200	9	-	6	-
300	20	1/2	14	-
400	40	1	28	1/2
500	68	1 1/2	48	1
600	100	2	70	1 1/2
700	150	3	105	2
800	210	4	147	3

Notes: 1. The aimpoint shift for strong wind (8 m/sec) is double, and for weak wind (2 m/sec)—one-half.

2. In a wind blowing at an angle of 30°, use 0.5 of the correction for a 90° wind; for a wind blowing at an angle of 60°, use 0.9 of the same correction.

3. Make the calculation for aimpoint shift from the center of the target (Figure 80).

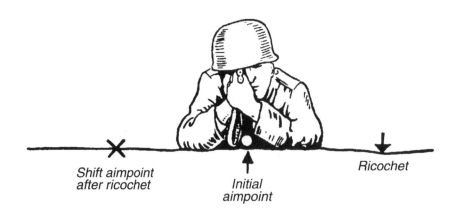

Shift aimpoint after ricochet

Initial aimpoint

Ricochet

Figure 80. Shift of aimpoint

171. In intense moments of combat, when there is not time to change the rear sight setting, conduct fire using the **battle sight range:**

    a) at running and exposed enemy (chest) targets–with the rear sight set at 4 for all ranges up to 400 meters, aiming at the waist of a running figure and under the target at a prone figure;

    b) at an enemy soldier in a trench (head target)–with the rear sight set at 3 for all ranges up to 300 meters, aiming under the target;

    c) at cavalry at all ranges up to 600 meters–with the rear sight set at 6, aiming under the chest of the horse.

172. The rifleman should select the most favorable moment for opening fire and not commence firing too soon.

The most favorable moments for opening fire are when the target can be defeated unexpectedly, when the target appears at full height or has exposed itself from behind cover, and when it is most visible.

Firing at Stationary Targets

173. Fire at individual exposed and stationary targets, selecting an aimpoint in accordance with paragraphs 167 and 168, with consideration for the influences of weather and wind.

Firing at Fleeting Targets

174. To defeat targets that appear for a brief time, it is necessary to observe the battlefield attentively, quickly recognize and evaluate targets, determine the range to them, and select the rear sight setting and aimpoint.

Rapid production of the shot at fleeting targets is achieved by rapid preparation.

175. To defeat fleeting targets, one must aim ahead of time at the spot where the target is expected to appear. Upon the target's appearance, rapidly refine the aim and make the shot.

When it is impossible to predict the place where the fleeting target will appear, destroy the target with a **snap shot**.

Firing at Moving Ground Targets

176. Conduct fire at a dismounted target moving in the plane of fire (at or away from the rifleman) with the rear sight set for the range at which the target might be at the moment the shot is fired. Set the rear sight at 1/2 – 1 markings less (greater).

177. To defeat targets moving on an angle to the plane of firing, set the rear sight at the range to the target, and shift the aimpoint in the direction of the target's movement, guided by the following table:

Firing range in meters	Running dismounted target (3 m/sec)				Running at a trot (4m/sec)		
	90° angle		45° angle		90°	45°	any angle
	aimpoint shift						
	cm	human forms	cm	human forms	cm	cm	visible human or horse figures
100	35	1/2	25	1/2	45	32	1/4
200	75	1 1/2	52	1	100	70	1/2
300	120	2 1/2	84	2	160	112	3/4
400	170	3 1/2	120	2 1/2	230	160	1 1/4
500	230	4 1/2	160	3	300	210	1 1/2
600	290	6	203	4	380	266	2
700	360	7	252	5	480	336	2 1/2
800	440	9	308	6	590	413	3

Notes: 1. For a walking dismounted target use one-half the correction required for a running target. For a walking horse, use one-half the correction required for a trotting horse; use twice the correction for a galloping horse.

2. For a dismounted target moving at an angle of 30°, use 0.5 of the correction for a moving target at 90°. For a target moving at an angle of 60°, use 0.9 of the same correction. Use the same factors for shifting the aimpoint in centimeters when firing at horse-mounted targets moving at angles of 30° and 60°.

3. Calculate the aimpoint shift from the center of the target.

178. When firing at a moving target, the rifleman can note a point along its path of movement and take aim at that point. When the target approaches that point at the magnitude of the necessary lead, fire the shot.

Firing at Armored Targets

179. Conduct rifle fire at armored targets (tanks, tankettes, armored cars) at vision ports with conventional bullets at ranges up to 200 meters, and at vital spots (motor, radiator, fuel cell, command positions) with special armor-piercing bullets up to 300 meters. If the target is moving laterally, shift the aimpoint along its movement path, guided by the following table:

Target speed in kph	Firing range		
	100	**200**	**300**
	lead in meters		
10	0.30	0.70	1.1
15	0.45	1.05	1.35
25	0.75	1.75	2.8

Note. This table is calculated on the movement of the armored target at a 90° angle. If the target is moving at a 60, 45, or 30° angle, use respectively 0.9, 0.7, and 0.5 of the correction shown in the table.

Firing at Aerial Targets

180. Rifle fire is conducted at aircraft and parachutists at ranges up to 500 meters with the rear sight set at 3.

181. The most favorable moment for firing at an aircraft is **when it is diving on the rifleman or departing after a dive**. In these cases conduct fire without applying lead, aiming at the nose of the diving aircraft and the tail of the departing aircraft.

182. In all other cases, apply a lead. The magnitude of the lead for aircraft moving at straight angles to the plane of firing is shown in the following table:

Aircraft speed in m/sec	Firing range and lead in meters				
	100	**200**	**300**	**400**	**500**
70	8.0	17.5	28.0	40.0	53.0
80	9.0	20.0	32.0	45.0	61.0
90	19.0	22.5	36.0	51.0	68.0
100	11.0	25.0	40.0	57.0	76.0
110	12.0	27.5	44.0	63.0	84.0
120	13.0	30.0	48.0	68.0	91.0
130	14.0	32.5	52.0	74.0	98.0
140	15.0	35.0	56.0	80.0	106.4
150	16.0	37.5	60.0	85.0	114.0

183. In a combat situation, guided by the table of leads in meters, assemble ahead of time a table of leads in enemy aircraft fuselages that are operating on a given axis, with consideration for their sizes and movement speeds. When firing take up a lead in visible fuselage forms (Figure 81), guided by the assembled table.

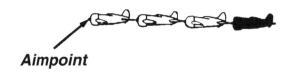

Aimpoint

Figure 81. firing at an aircraft passing across the front

Example. The speed of an aircraft is 80 m/sec [180 mph]. The length of its fuselage is 10 meters. Shift the aimpoint 1 fuselage length at 100 meters firing range, 2 fuselage lengths at 200 meters, 3 fuselage lengths at 300 meters, 4.5 fuselage lengths at 400 meters, and 6 fuselage lengths at 500 meters.

184. Conduct fire at aircraft using conventional or special bullets. Use cartridges with tracer bullets for adjusting fire, having loaded them into the rifle alternated with conventional or special cartridges. Commence firing at aircraft upon command of the squad commander.

185. When firing at descending parachutists, shift the aimpoint in the direction of fall. Apply a lead in visible forms of the parachutist, as indicated in the table and Figure 82.

Firing range in meters	100	200	300	400	500
Shift of aimpoint in visible parachutist forms at descent rate of 6 m/sec	under the feet	1/2	1	1 1/2	2 1/2

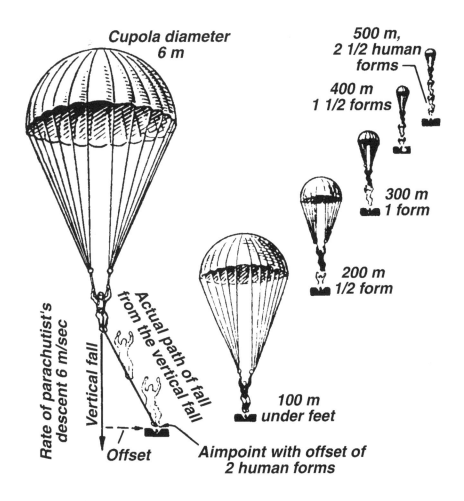

Figure 82. Firing at a parachutist

186. The position of the rifleman for firing at aerial targets is arbitrary, depending on the terrain and situation–sitting, kneeling, prone or standing, any position that provides the necessary stability and flexibility (Figures 83, 84, 85). Low local objects–fences, tree stumps, and so on, can be used for support during firing.

Figure 83. Firing at aerial targets in the kneeling position

Figure 84. Firing at aerial targets in the standing position

Figure 85. Firing at aerial targets in chemical protective clothing

Firing in Mountains

187. When firing in mountains, the range of flight of the bullet is increased relative to flat terrain as a consequence of the reduced air density, depending on the altitude above sea level. Make the necessary corrections for this, guided by the following table.

Firing range in meters	Altitude of terrain above sea level in meters											
	500	1000	1500	2000	2500	3000	500	1000	1500	2000	2500	3000
	lower aimpoint (in centimeters)						reduce sight setting (in rear sight markings)					
500	5	10	10	15	20	25	-	-	-	1/2	1/2	1/2
600	10	25	35	45	55	70	-	-	1/2	1/2	1/2	1/2
700	20	40	60	80	95	115	-	1/2	1/2	1/2	1	1
800	30	70	110	140	170	205	-	1/2	1/2	1	1	1

Significant angles of the target location also influence the change in the range of the flight of the bullet when firing in mountains.

Make corrections for the influence of significant angles of the target location in rear sight markings, guided by the following table:

Firing range in meters (slant range)	100	200	300	400	500	600	700	800
Angle of target location in degrees	Corrections in rear sight markings: increase sight setting with + decrease sight setting with –							
–35	-	–1/2	–1/2	–1/2	–1/2	–1/2	–1/2	–1/2
–30	-	-	–1/2	–1/2	–1/2	–1/2	–1/2	–1/2
–25	-	-	-	-	-	-	–1/2	–1/2
–20	-	-	-	-	-	-	-	-
–15	-	-	-	-	-	-	-	-
–10	-	-	-	-	-	-	-	-
–5	-	-	-	-	-	-	-	-
0	-	-	-	-	-	-	-	-
+5	-	-	-	-	-	-	+1/2	+1/2
+10	-	-	-	-	-	+1/2	+1/2	+1/2
+15	-	-	-	-	-	+1/2	+1/2	+1/2
+20	-	-	-	-	-	-	-	+1/2
+25	-	-	-	-	-	-	-	-
+30	-	-	-	-	-	-	-	-
+35	-	–1/2	–1/2	–1/2	–1/2	-	-	-
+40	-	–1/2	–1/2	–1/2	–1/2	–1/2	–1/2	–1/2
+45	–1/2	–1/2	–1/2	–1/2	–1/2	–1/2	–1	–1
+50	–1/2	–1/2	–1	–1	–1	–1	–1	–1

Note. The table presents approximate numbers. When firing it is necessary to observe the results of the fire and, if required, make corrections.

188. Normal firing methods are not always applicable when firing in mountains. Therefore, the rifleman should adapt to the terrain, particularly when firing at large angles from above to below or from below upward. It may be more suitable to fire from a support.

Firing at Camouflaged and Concealed Targets

189. To defeat a target concealed behind camouflage (grass, bush, branches, and so on), conduct fire at the camouflage at the point where the target is located. If the position of the target behind the camouflage is unknown, fire at the camouflage and shift the aimpoint in half-meter increments.

190. If an insignificant obstacle prevents the rifleman from seeing the target (bush, dirt parapet, grass, and so on), and the rifleman is unable to change his firing position, he can raise up slightly and seek out the target above the obstacle. Then, slowly dropping his head to the stock, he can note an aimpoint on the obstacle where the target is located. This noted aimpoint is a **subsidiary aimpoint** for firing.

Firing in Limited Visibility Conditions

191. Firing at night at illuminated targets is conducted by the same regulations as during the day. At the moment of illumination the rifleman should quickly take aim and fire the shot. Upon illumination of the targets, avoid looking at the illumination means (flares, searchlight) so as not to be blinded by the light.

The determination of range, even during strong artificial illumination, is extremely difficult at night. Therefore the ranges to the places at which the appearance of targets is possible should be determined during daylight.

192. Firing at night without artificial illumination (and also firing in fog and smoke) can be successful only with prior preparation. To accomplish this, make use of the following devices:

a) make a **channel** in the trench parapet for laying and maintaining the required direction of the rifle (Figure 86). If time permits, pack the channel down and cover it with sod.

Figure 86.

b) plant two pairs of **limiting stakes** in the parapet for each rifle. Place the front pair near the upper barrel band and the rear pair near the stock or magazine (Figure 87). **Forked wood sticks** can be used in place of the pairs of stakes (Figure 88).

Figure 87.

Figure 88.

Lay the rifle so that during firing at a range of 100–200 meters the line of sight passes not more than one-half meter above the ground.

193. If preparation for firing in limited visibility conditions has not been conducted ahead of time, open fire only to defeat an assault.

194. If it is necessary to fire through a smoke screen without preliminary preparation, fire directly at the smoke screen as though it were camouflage (paragraph 189).

Firing in Conditions of Chemical Contamination

195. The peculiarities of firing in a protective mask are: misting of eyepieces from breathing that disrupts clear visibility of the target, and some constraining of breathing.

Use special pencils [a kind of applicator for a palliative substance, similar to a camouflage stick] to prevent misting of eyepieces. To become accustomed to working for long periods in a protective mask and not experience great discomfort or difficulty in breathing, it is necessary to train regularly in firing with the protective mask on.

When firing in the protective mask, the eyepiece in front of the dominant eye should be perpendicular to the plane of vision.

Firing on the Move

196. Firing can be conducted on the move by making snap shots at short halts or without stopping.

To fire a **snap shot from a short halt**, stop movement when the left foot strikes the ground and, without extending the right leg, quickly shoulder the rifle so that the line of sight is pointed at the target. Fire the shot and then continue movement, reloading the rifle on the move.

To fire a **snap shot without stopping**, quickly shoulder the rifle when the right foot strikes the ground. Having brought the line of sight to the target, make the shot when the left foot strikes the ground, continuing movement while reloading for subsequent firing.

When moving in the assault, conduct fire without stopping movement, using snap shots or pointing the rifle with the left arm at the enemy, and holding the stock into the side with the right arm.

In an unanticipated encounter with the enemy, defeat him with a quick point-blank shot from any position, pointing the rifle's muzzle at the target.

Ammunition Supply in Combat

197. The rifleman carries a supply of cartridges in belt and spare pouches and in the rucksack.

The rifleman should keep track of his ammunition expenditure in the course of battle and when one-half of his ammunition has been fired, report this to the squad commander.

198. Each rifleman is required, without relying on timely delivery of cartridges from the rear, to look after the replenishment of his own supply, picking up cartridges discarded on the battlefield and also taking them from the wounded and dead.

199. Each soldier should hold on to one package [15 rounds] of cartridges as an untouchable supply that can be expended only with the commander's permission.

Appendix 1

Firing Tables

Magnitude of trajectory over line of sight for type-1908 bullet fired from rifle

Range in meters	50	100	150	200	250	300	350	400	450
Sight setting	measured in centimeters								
1	3	0	−5						
2	6	7	6	0	−10				
3	10	17	20	19	12	0	−18		
4	16	28	37	40	40	32	20	0	−27

Range in meters	100	200	300	400	500	600	700	800	900	1000
Sight setting	measured in meters									
5	0.3	0.6	0.7	0.5	0	−0.8	−2.2			
6	0.5	1.0	1.2	1.1	0.8	0	−1.2	−3.0		
7	0.7	1.4	1.7	1.8	1.7	1.2	0	−1.6	−4.2	
8	0.9	1.8	2.3	2.7	2.7	2.4	1.5	−0	−2.2	−5.4

Note. Numbers with minus sign indicate magnitude of trajectory below line of sight.

Magnitude of trajectory over line of sight for type-1908 bullet fired from carbine

Range in meters	50	100	150	200	250	300	350	400	450
Sight setting	measured in centimeters								
1	2	0	−3						
2	6	8	8	0	−14				
3	11	19	23	21	14	0	−20		
4	17	31	40	45	43	35	20	0	−33

Range in meters	100	200	300	400	500	600	700	800	900	1000
Sight setting	measured in meters									
5	0.5	0.8	0.9	0.6	0	−1.0				
6	0.7	1.2	1.4	1.3	0.9	0	−1.4			
7	0.9	1.6	2.0	2.1	1.9	1.2	0	−2.1		
8	1.1	2.1	2.8	3.1	3.1	2.8	1.8	−0	−2.9	

Table of angles of elevation, drift, and time of flight of type-1908 bullet

Firing range in meters	Elevation angle in mils		Drift in centimeters	Bullet time of flight in seconds	
	rifle	carbine		rifle	carbine
100	2.2	3.3	-	0.11	0.13
200	2.8	3,9	-	0.25	0.28
300	3.6	4.7	2	0.40	0.44
400	4.7	5.8	4	0.57	0.62
500	6.1	7.2	7	0.76	0.82
600	7.5	8.9	12	0.97	1.04
700	9.2	11.0	19	1.21	1.29
800	11.0	13.0	29	1.47	1.57

Appendix 2

Comparative Weight and Length Data for the Rifle and Carbines

Data	Rifle type 1891/30	Carbine type 1938	Carbine type 1944
Total weight–with bayonet, without cartridges, in kg/lb	4.5/9.9	–	3.9/8.6
Total weight–without bayonet and cartridges, in kg/lb	4.0/8.8	3.7/7.7	–
Weight of bayonet in kg/oz	0.5/18	–	0.4/14
Total length with bayonet (in combat position) in cm/in	166/65	–	133/52
Total length without bayonet (in travel position) in cm/in	123/48	102/40	102/40
Length of bayonet blade (from muzzle) in cm/in	43/17	–	31/12
Length of barrel (with chamber) in mm/in	730/28.7	512/20.1	517/20.3
Length of rifled portion of barrel in mm/in	657/25.9	493/17.3	444/17.5
Number of lands	4	4	4
Caliber of barrel bore in mm	7.62	7.62	7.62
Length of sight plane in mm/in	622/24.5	416/16.4	416/16.4
Height of front sight above bore line in mm/in	23.6/.93	23.1/.91	23.1/.91
Weight of charger clip with cartridges in g/oz	122–132/4.3–4.7	122–132/4.3–4.7	122–132/4.3–4.7
Weight of cartridge with iron case in g/oz	21–23/.74–.81	21–23/.74–.81	21–23/.74–.81
Weight of cartridge with brass case in g/oz	22–24/.78–.85	22–24/.78–.85	22–24/.78–.85
Propellant weight in g/grains	3.25/50	3.25/50	3.25/50
Projectile (type-1908) weight in g/grains	9.6/148	9.6/148	9.6/148
Muzzle velocity of projectile in m/sec//fps	865//2838	820//2690	820//2690

Appendix 3

Optical Sight [scope]

1. The optical sight for the sniper rifle facilitates precise aiming at various targets, of especially small size and which appear for a brief time. The sight permits the conduct of precision fire and during unfavorable conditions of illumination (at dusk and dawn), when it is difficult to fire at targets using the iron sights.

2. Two optical sights are in the inventory–PE and PU (Figures 89 and 90).

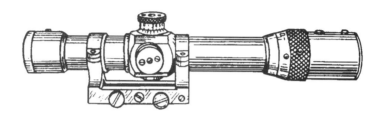

Figure 89. General view of the PE scope and mount

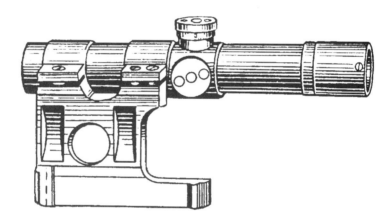

Figure 90. General view of the PU scope and mount

Both scopes consist of an optical tube of constant magnification and a mount.

3. The optical tube has externally:
    a) on top–a drum with knob and scale marked in 100-meter increments for setting the elevation angle (the PE scope has scale markings from 1 to 14, and the PU scope from 1 to 13);
    b) on the left side–a drum for windage corrections (calculation of wind, drift and shift of aimpoint during firing at moving targets). The scale of the lateral drum is marked in 10 deflection markings in both directions from zero: with a + (plus) sign for corrections to the right and a – (minus) sign for corrections to the left. Only the 5th and 10th increments are marked. The value of each mark is 1/1000th of the range [1 mil].

4. Contained inside the tube is a frame with aiming filaments (the reticule). The vertical filament with the pointed end is called the sight post and serves to align the top of the sight post with the aimpoint.

The horizontal filaments are positioned at right angles to the post with their upper edges at the same height as the pointed end of the vertical post. They are intended to assist the rifleman in holding the rifle level during aiming.

The frame with aiming filaments can be moved up and down by rotation of the upper drum, and to the right or left by rotation of the lateral drum.

Inside the scope tube is an optical system consisting of the objective lens, rotation system, and ocular lens (Figure 91).

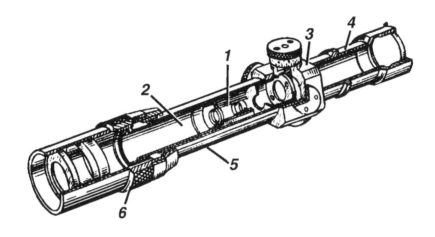

Figure 91. Optical sight PE in cutaway

1 - rotation lens	2 - inner tube	3 - body
4 - objective tube	5 - outer tube	6 - intermediate tube

The objective lens system consists of two lenses glued together.

The rotational system consists of four lenses glued in pairs.

The ocular system consists of three lenses, two of which are glued together.

On the tube the PE scope has a knurled ring and scale with markings for adjusting the scope to the eye: with the + (plus) sign for far-sighted shooters and the – (minus) sign for near-sighted shooters.

5. Reflected light from the viewed object enters the scope through the objective system, which gives a reverse (turned upside down and right-to-left) reduced image.

The rotation system is designed to correct the image provided by the objective system and provide a direct (turned rightside up and from left-to-right) reduced image.

When aiming, the rifleman sees through the ocular lens (as through a magnifying glass) the corrected image produced by the objective system, direct and magnified, which ensures great accuracy in aiming.

6. The adjustment of the PE scope to the eyes is accomplished by rotation of the knurled ring. Adjustment of the PU scope is accomplished by the rifleman bringing his eye closer or moving it farther away from the ocular lens until he achieves the best view through the scope.

Construction of the Mount for the PE Scope

7. The mount serves to secure the scope to the rifle.

The mount base (Figure 92) is tightly secured by six screws on the forward portion of the receiver.

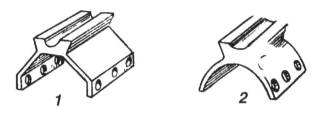

Figure 92. Mount base for PE scope

1 - for faceted receiver   2 - for round receiver

On top of the mount base is a longitudinal **rail** onto which the scope mount fits. The **mount** consists of two segments–**lower** and **upper** (Figure 93).

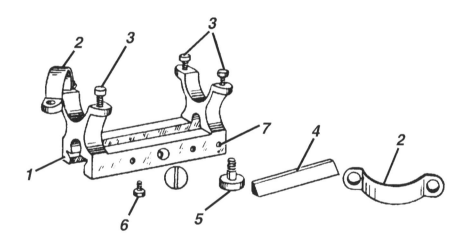

Figure 93. Mount for PE scope

1 - lower segment   2 - upper segment   3 - half-ring screws
4 - wedge   5 - tension screws   6 - wedge screw
7 - mounting screw

The **lower segment** is for mounting the scope. It has **two stanchions** with grooves and flanges with holes for screws and a **longitudinal channel**, the right wall of which is beveled. The stanchions of the mount have **windows** for firing with the iron sights without removing the scope.

The **wedge** is housed in the channel of the mount. On the left side in the lower portion of the mount are **two threaded holes** for tension screws, one smooth hole for the wedge screw, and another for the screw that secures the lower portion of the mount to the rail. A hole has also been made in the right side of the mount for this purpose. The **insert** limits movement of the mount on the base.

With the help of the tension screws, the **mount wedge** draws together the beveled edge of the channel of the lower portion of the mount to the beveled edge of the sight base rail. The wedge has a threaded **hole** for the screw that keeps the wedge from falling out of the lower portion of the mount when the mount is removed from the base.

The **tension screws** have knurling on their heads for tightening them by hand and a slot for tightening with a screwdriver.

The **upper segment of the mount** consists of two half-rings with flanges and holes for the screws that secure the scope in the mount.

On the base and lower portion of the mount (on the right side) is inscribed a serial number that is common with the rifle.

Construction of the Type-1942 Mount for the PU Scope

8.   The mount serves as an attachment point for the scope and connects the scope with the sniper rifle. The mount consists of a base and a body.

9.   The body, including the optical tube of the scope, is secured to the **mount base**. The base is tightly attached to the left side of the receiver by two pins, and two screws that are prevented from coming unscrewed by locking screws (Figure 94).

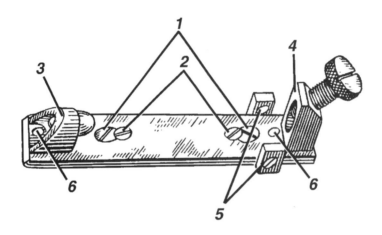

Figure 94. Mount base for PU scope

1 - attaching screws   2 - locking screws
3 - stanchion with pivot ball   4 - stanchion with tension screw
5 - flanges with regulating screws   6 - pins

On the front portion of the mount base is a stanchion with ball pivot, and on the rear portion a stanchion with tension screw for joining and securing the body of the mount.

Near the rear stanchion are **two flanges with regulating screws**, the use of which (for adjusting the scope) is authorized only in special repair facilities.

10. The **mount body** (Figure 95) serves to secure the scope and to adjust it when confirming the rifle's zero.

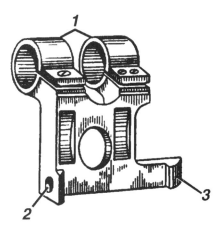

Figure 95. Mount body for PU scope

1 - clamps   2 - ball receptacle   3 - projection

On its upper portion it has two **collars** which hold the scope **tube**. A single screw tightens the front collar and two screws the rear collar. On the front portion of the body is a **ball receptacle** for joining the body with the mount base.

On the left side of the rear portion is a **projection with tapered area**, by which the body fits to the mount base.

11. The mount base is not removed from the receiver. Attached mount bodies with scope tubes are not subject to disassembly in troop units, and can only be removed from the mount base when required by unit conditions.

12. The mount is removed from the base by the following method: unscrew the tension screw from the stanchion until it no longer emerges from the face of the stanchion. Remove the mount body along with the scope tube from the base with hand effort. When installing the mount on the base, place the ball receptacle on the pivot ball of the mount base. Insert the tail portion of the body between the regulating screws. Secure the mount body with the tension screws using a screwdriver.

Bringing the Sniper Rifle to a Normal Zero by a Proof Firer

13. Before the rifle is issued to a sniper, it is check fired and brought to a normal zero with the iron sights using a special registration bench [rest or vise].

Confirmation of zero is accomplished by a proof firer in accordance with the regulations contained in Chapter 5 of these Instructions, with the following changes and supplements:

a) confirmation of the rifle's zero is conducted without the bayonet and with the scope installed;

b) the rifle's zero is recognized as normal if the holes of all four bullets are contained in a circle of 8 centimeters diameter, with the mean point of impact of those four holes at a control point located 17 centimeters above the aimpoint;

c) the horizontal position of the rear sight aperture piece is checked for level when the rifle is secured to the bench (by eye in extreme circumstances);

14. Upon completion of zero confirmation of the rifle with iron sights, the scope is **adjusted** on the bench.

a) lay the rifle by the iron sights on an aimpoint and, without changing the lay, rotate the top drum to align the elevation adjustment knob with the number 3, and the windage adjustment knob with the number 0.

b) look through the scope to determine where the reticule is resting. If it is on the aimpoint, the optical sight is properly adjusted.

If the line of sight of the scope does not lie on the aimpoint, rotate the knobs in the appropriate direction without disturbing the lay of the rifle on the bench to bring the line of sight to the aimpoint. After this has been accomplished, loosen the drum screws of the elevation and windage knobs approximately one–two turns, without moving the knobs themselves. Rotate the rings so that the mark with the number 3 is aligned with the index mark on the elevation drum and the number 0 is aligned with the index mark on the windage drum. Confirm that the reticule did not shift when the rings were moved, and carefully tighten the drum screws. In the event the reticule moved, tighten the drum screws and adjust the sight again as instructed above.

Inclination of the optical tube (the horizontal reticules of the sight have inclined relative to the rear sight aperture piece) is corrected by an armaments specialist.

Bringing the Sniper Rifle to a Normal Zero by the Sniper

15. The sniper brings the rifle to a normal zero with both the iron sights and optical sight after the rifle is issued to him.

16. Bringing the rifle to a normal zero with iron sights is conducted in accordance with the regulations contained in Chapter 5 of these Instructions, with the following changes and supplements:

a) confirmation of the rifle's zero is conducted without the bayonet, with optical sight installed;

b) confirmation of zero is accomplished from the prone position using a support;

c) the rifle's zero is evaluated for shot group size and accuracy as instructed in paragraph 13 of this appendix.

17. Bringing the sniper rifle to a normal zero with the **optical sight** is conducted in accordance with the instructions indicated above, and with observation of the following conditions:

a) firing is conducted with the upper [elevation] drum set at the number 3 and the lateral [windage] drum set at 0;

b) confirmation of zero is considered completed if all four bullet holes are contained in a circle of 8 centimeters diameter, with the mean point of impact of those four holes at a control point located 17 centimeters above the aimpoint.

If, as a consequence of deviation of the mean point of impact, the holes of all four bullets are not contained in a control circle of 8 centimeters diameter, firing is repeated with appropriate changes to the settings of the knobs.

For seeking the necessary setting of the upper drum during repeat firing, use the table of elevation angles.

Example. During firing at 100 meters and with the upper drum set at 3, the mean point of impact is located above the control point by 8 centimeters, that is, 0.8 mils.

The table of elevation angles [the third table at Appendix 1] shows that the sight setting of 3 [300 meters] corresponds to an elevation angle of 3.6 mils, and a sight setting of 2 [200 meters] corresponds to an elevation angle of 2.8 mils. It is necessary to reduce the elevation angle by 0.8 mils. Consequently, when firing the second series of shots, it is necessary to place the number 2 of the upper drum at the index mark. When firing is conducted at this setting, the mean point of impact should coincide with the control point.

Changing the position of the mean point of impact in the lateral direction is accomplished by a corresponding change to the setting of the windage drum. One marking of this drum changes the location of the mean point of impact by 10 centimeters at 100 meters.

18. If all four bullets fall in a circle of 8 centimeters diameter when firing is conducted with the elevation knob set at a number greater or less than 3, and the windage knob not at 0, one must:

a) loosen the upper and lateral knob screws approximately one–two turns;

b) without touching the drums, rotate only the rings far enough to align the number 3 with the index on the elevation drum and the number 0 with the index on the windage drum;

c) tighten the drum screws.

The scope reticule should not be shifted when rotating the rings. Fire a series of control shots in order to confirm this. If the mean point of impact does not coincide with the control point, repeat the confirmation as instructed above.

19. The sniper rifle should be brought to a normal zero:

a) after 150 to 200 shots have been fired;

b) every time the scope is removed from the rifle;

c) upon loosening of the screws of the mount base or the PE scope rings, or upon loosening of the screws of the base and body of the PU scope mount;

d) upon reissue of the rifle to another sniper.

Storage and Preservation of the Scope for the Sniper Rifle

20. Disassembly of the scope is not permitted in troop units.

21. Removal of the scope with mount from the rifle during movement, cleaning, and storage of the rifle is prohibited.

22. Protect the scope from falls, sharp blows, jarring, and penetration of moisture and dust into its internal parts.

23. Store the optical sight in dry heated surroundings with a temperature not less than +5–6 C° [43° F].

24. Remove the canvas bag and lens end caps only before commencing fire, inspection, and cleaning of the scope.

25. Before installing the lens caps and canvas bag, inspect the scope and wipe its lenses with a clean, well-washed rag, which has been shaken to remove dust. Hold the scope vertically. Remove dust and small hard particles from the lenses with a soft, dry rag or brush. Wipe the lenses with a circular motion, beginning with the middle of the lens. Shake out the rag frequently.

26. Carefully wipe the exterior surface of a wet scope with a dry cloth. Dry the canvas bag and end caps.

27. When cleaning the rifle, lightly lubricate the metal components of the scope with an oiled rag.

28. Do not put lubricant on the lenses or touch them with the fingers.

29. Do not rotate the elevation and windage knobs unless it is necessary to do so.
    When setting the scope knobs at the required markings, and also when adjusting the PE scope by eye, rotate the drums and ring smoothly, without sharp movement and pressure.

Inspection of the Sniper Rifle

30. Inspection of sniper rifles is accomplished in accordance with regulations contained in Chapter 4 of these Instructions. In addition, check to ensure:
    a) the objective and ocular lenses are intact;
    b) for the PE scope–the scope mount and base screws are tight. If the screws are tightened correctly, the base should not wiggle on the receiver, the mount should not wiggle on the base, and the scope should not wiggle in the mount. For the PU scope—the screws for the mount base and body are tight. If the screws are tightened correctly, the mount base should not wiggle on the receiver, the body should not wiggle on the mount, and the scope should not wiggle in the half-rings. If any screws are loose, tighten them a bit at a time and carefully.
    Note. In order more easily to detect mount screws that have become loose and correctly return them to their previous position, it is recommended to record the position of the screw head slots in the shooter's logbook.
    c) For the PE scope–the locking rings are present on the ocular lens system, on the moving ring, and on the fixed ring with index mark. The ocular and objective tubes are secured by the stop rings on the scope body, the objective mounting is secured on the objective tube and the knobs with scales by their screws. For the PU scope–the locking ring is present on the ocular mounting and the knobs with scales are secured by their screws;
    d) the drums and their scales do not wiggle;
    e) the drums and knurled ring rotate properly;
    f) there is no dirt on the lenses; the reticule is in proper position and shifts when the drums are rotated (check through the ocular lens).

Adjusting the Scope to the Eye (for Clarity)

31. To adjust the PE scope to the eye:

    a) remove the leather covers from the objective and ocular lenses;

    b) secure the rifle on a bench and lay it on an object with regular and sharp features, located not closer than 200 meters;

    c) rotate the knurled ring until the image of the object and the scope reticule are sharp and clear;

    d) look to see what marking on the ring is at the index line;

    e) position the 0 marking at the index line and again adjust the scope to the eyes as indicated above.

If the mark on the ring at the index line is the same in both tries, the scope was adjusted properly to the eyes. If the marking is different, go through the adjustment process several times and take the average.

Upon subsequent work with the scope, immediately set the ring at the proper mark.

When adjusting the scope to the eye, hold the eye approximately 8 centimeters from the ocular lens.

Adjusting the PU scope to the eye is accomplished by bringing the rifleman's eye closer to or farther away from the outer ocular lens until the image of the object and the scope reticule are sharp and clear. When this is achieved, the eye should be approximately 65 to 80 millimeters [2.5 to 3 inches] from the ocular lens.

Descriptive Data for the Optical Sights

	scope system	
	PE	PU
Magnification	4-power	3.5-power
Field of view	5°30'	4°30'
Diameter of exit pupil (mm/in)	7/.28	6/.24
Length of exit pupil (mm/in)	83/3.3	72/2.8
Length (mm/in)	274/10.8	169/6.7
Weight (g/oz)	598/21	270/9.5

Firearms Safety

The Mosin-Nagant Rifle is a firearm and a dangerous weapon. It is potentially lethal.

WARNING: If the Mosin-Nagant rifle, or any firearm, is carelessly or improperly handled, unintentional discharge could result and could cause injury, death, or damage to property.

Users of Mosin-Nagant rifles are advised to carefully read the instruction manual if one came with the firearm, prior to loading and firing. Your safety and the safety of others, including members of your family, depends on your understanding and mature compliance with the applicable instruction manual and your constant use of safe firearms handling practices. If you are unfamiliar with firearms, seek further advice through safe handling courses offered by local gun clubs, National Rifle Association approved instructors, or similar qualified organizations.

Russian Military Translations and Enterprise Design and Publishing shall not be responsible for injury, death, or damage to property resulting from either intentional or unintentional discharge of a Mosin-Nagant rifle.

Six Basic Firearms Safety Rules

1. Never put a round in the chamber until you are ready to shoot.

2. Always point the gun in a safe direction.

3. Keep the selector on safe until you are ready to fire.

4. Unload the weapon completely immediately after use, and double check the chamber.

5. Always ensure a gun is not loaded before cleaning or disassembling it.

6. Practice handling the gun empty before attempting to load and fire it.

WARNING: When you squeeze the trigger of any firearm, you must expect the firearm to fire, and you must take full responsibility for firing it. Your careful handling can avoid accidental discharge, and you can avoid accidental injury and death.

WARNING: This firearm may accidentally fire when a round is loaded into the chamber, if the firearm is dropped, or receives a blow to the muzzle or front of the gun. This can occur regardless of the hammer or safety positions. Extra care and strict use of safe handling procedures by the firearm user is mandatory and essential to minimize risk of accidents.

Firearms Safe Handling Rules

- Always handle your firearm as if it were loaded, so that you never fire it accidentally when you think it is unloaded.

- Never point your firearm at anything you do not want to shoot, so that if it fires accidentally, you will prevent injury, death, or damage to property.

- Never take anyone's word that a firearm is unloaded. Check for yourself with your fingers off the trigger and the gun pointed in a safe direction, so that you never fire the firearm accidentally when you think it is unloaded.

- Always make sure your firearm is not loaded and the slide or bolt is latched open before laying it down, or handing it to another person, so that it cannot be fired accidentally or when it is unsafe to fire it.

- Always keep and carry your firearm empty, with the hammer forward except when you intend to shoot, so that your firearm cannot be fired when you do not mean to fire it.

- Always be aware of possible risk from dropping your firearm. Some parts of the mechanism could be damaged. You may not see the damage, but if it is severe, the firearm may discharge and cause injury, death, or damage to property. If your firearm has been dropped, have it examined by a competent gunsmith before using it again.

- Never leave a firearm cocked ready to fire. This condition is extremely dangerous, and the firearm could easily be accidentally discharged, causing injury, death, or damage to property.

- Never leave a loaded firearm unattended. Someone, especially a child, may fire it and cause injury, death, or damage to property.

- Store your firearms and ammunition securely locked and in separate locations out of reach and sight of children. Children are naturally curious and do not always recognize or believe the real danger of guns.

- Always instruct children and others in your home to respect firearms. If you teach your children to shoot, teach them or get them trained by a qualified instructor to treat and use the firearm properly. Always supervise them closely. Always stress safety so that your children will not fire the firearm when it is unsafe to do so.

- Always be sure your shooting backstop is adequate to stop and contain bullets before beginning target practice, so that you do not hit anything outside the range shooting area.

- Always put a knowledgeable and responsible adult in charge to maintain safety control when a group is firing on a range. Obey his or her commands to maintain discipline and reduce the possibility of accidents.

- Always carry your firearm empty with the bolt latched open or slide locked open while on a range until preparing to fire. Keep it pointing toward the backstop when loading, firing, and unloading, to eliminate the risk of injury, death, or damage to property from premature or accidental discharge.

- Always be sure the barrel, bore, chamber, and action are clean and clear of obstructions. Clean a wet or fouled firearm immediately so that it will function correctly and safely.

- Always use only clean, dry, original, high quality, commercially manufactured ammunition in good condition that is appropriate to the caliber of your firearm. Gun and ammunition manufacturers design their products within exacting engineering safety limits. Handloads and remanufactured ammunition are sometimes outside of those limits and can be so unsafe as to explode in the chamber and receiver to cause injury, death, or damage to property. The use of remanufactured or hand loaded ammunition is not recommended.

- Always check that ammunition is clean and undamaged. Do not force ammunition into the chamber. Forcing damaged ammunition into the chamber could damage your firearm and could result in injury, death, or damage to property.

- Never drink alcoholic beverages or take drugs before or during shooting, as your vision and judgment could be seriously impaired, making your gun handling unsafe.

- Always seek a doctor's advice if you are taking medication, to be sure that neither your condition nor your medication render you unfit to shoot and handle your firearm safely.

- Always wear and encourage others to wear ear protection when shooting, especially on a range. Without ear protection, the noise from your firearm and other guns close to you could leave a "ringing" in the ears for some time after firing. Temporary and permanent hearing loss can result from unprotected exposure to noise from firearms.

- Always wear and encourage others to wear protective shooting glasses. Flying particles could damage your eyes and cause blindness. Protective glasses designed for shooting should prevent such injury. Ensure protective glasses are designed for protection while shooting firearms.

- Always keep the safety selector switch set to "safe" when the firearm is loaded and cocked, until you are aiming at your target and intend to fire. This will reduce the risk of accidental firing.

- If your firearm fails to fire when you pull the trigger, hold it, keeping it pointed toward the target, and wait 30 seconds. If a hang fire (slow ignition) has occurred, the round should fire within 30 seconds. If the round does not fire within 30 seconds, remove the magazine, eject the round and examine the primer. If the firing pin indent on the primer is light, misaligned, or non-existent, have a competent gunsmith examine your firearm. If the firing pin indent on the primer appears normal in comparison with previously fired rounds, assume faulty ammunition. Segregate misfired rounds from other live ammunition and empty cases. Reload and continue firing. Dispose of misfired rounds in accordance with the ammunition manufacturer's instructions.

- Never use your firearm if it fails to operate properly. Never force a jammed round, as a round may explode causing serious injury, possible death, or severe damage to your firearm.

- Always keep clear and keep others clear of the cartridge ejection port. Spent cartridges are ejected with enough force to cause injury, and the ejection port must be clear to ensure safe ejection of spent cartridges or live rounds. Never place your fingers in the ejection area. You could be burned by hot metal or injured by the bolt or slide moving forward.

- Never put your finger inside the trigger guard or squeeze the trigger until you are aiming at a target and are ready to shoot. This will prevent you from firing the firearm when it is pointing in an unsafe direction.

- Always be absolutely sure of your target, and the area around and behind it, before you squeeze the trigger. A bullet could travel miles beyond your target. If in doubt, don't shoot.

- Never attempt to fire with water in the barrel. Water can accumulate if your firearm is exposed to heavy rain or fog. Open the bolt or slide and allow the water to drain. Clean and dry the weapon before firing, if possible.

- Never shoot at a hard surface such as a rock, or a liquid surface such as water. A bullet may ricochet and travel in any direction to strike you, or an object you cannot see, causing injury, death, or damage to property.

- Never fire your firearm near an animal unless the animal is trained to accept the noise. An animal's startled reaction could injure it or cause an accident.

- Never indulge in "horseplay" while holding your firearm, or with anyone else holding a firearm, as it may be accidentally discharged.

- Never walk, climb, or follow a companion with your firearm cocked ready to fire. To eliminate the risk of accidental discharge, hold your firearm so that you can always control the direction of the muzzle, and keep the safety selector lever set to "safe."

- Always make sure your firearm is not loaded before cleaning or storing it, so that it cannot be fired when it is unsafe to do so.

- When disassembling or assembling a firearm, wear safety glasses in case you lose control of a spring or spring-loaded component that could injure your eyes.

- Never abuse your firearm by using it for any purpose other than shooting.

- Never dry fire the firearm when the receiver is open, and do not alter parts, as the level of safety could be reduced.

Various federal, state, and local laws govern the transfer and transportation of firearms. If you do not know the applicable laws, consult a firearms dealer or a law enforcement official in your area prior to transferring or transporting any firearm.

If there is anything you do not understand regarding use and operation of the Mosin-Nagant rifle or any firearm, seek advice from someone qualified in the safe handling of firearms.

This instruction manual is intended only as a historical reference document. It was originally published in Russian by the Ministry of Defense of the Union of Soviet Socialist Republics Military Press in 1961 as an instruction manual for their military personnel on the use and maintenance of the Mosin-Nagant Rifle. Although careful study of this translation could be potentially beneficial to anyone who owns or uses these firearms, this translation is not intended to be an owner's or operator's safety and instruction manual for the Mosin-Nagant rifle.